after
THE END

Teaching and Learning Creative Revision

Barry Lane

Heinemann
Portsmouth, New Hampshire

Heinemann
A division of Reed Elsevier Inc.
361 Hanover Street   Portsmouth, NH 03801-3912
Offices and agents throughout the world

Every effort has been made to contact the students and copyright holders for
permission to reprint borrowed material. We regret any oversights that may
have occurred and would be happy to rectify them in future printings of this
work.

Library of Congress Cataloging-in-Publication Data
Lane, Barry, 1955-
    After the end : teaching and learning creative revision / Barry
Lane.
        p.   cm.
    Includes bibliographical references and index.
    ISBN 0-435-08714-2
    1. English language—Composition and exercises—Study and teaching
(Elementary) 2. English language—Composition and exercises—Study
and teaching (Secondary)   I. Title.
    LB1576.L27   1992
808'.042'0712—dc20   92-32704
                                                          CIP

**For information about seminars and in-service workshops by Barry Lane,
call toll free 1–800–613–8055.**

Back cover photo by Robert Eddy of Randolf, VT.

Appearing in back-cover photo with the author are Melanie Ingalls (left) and
Sarah MacAskill (right).

Designed by Maria Szmauz.
Printed in the United States of America.
02 01   RRD   15 16 17 18 19 20

For Jessie Lynn, Grace Shoshana, and Abigail Anne

In Memory of Thomas Williams

...of making books
there is no end.
Ecclesiastes 12:12

contents

Creating a Language of Craft   part one

The Writer's Struggle   p a r t   t w o

acknowledgments

All books are adventures. This one started in a phone conversation with Dawn Boyer at Heinemann. I remain deeply indebted to Dawn for telling me what I said. Her lucid vision, guidance, and good humor at all stages of the project helped to shape this book. What a joy it is to have an editor who is also a writer and a friend.

I am also indebted to production editor Nancy Sheridan, whose fine work helped make the practical ideas in this book come through, and to Maria Szmauz for her elegant design.

At the time of writing the book I was an artist-in-residence at Vermont schools too numerous to mention. I'd like to thank all those teachers and students I worked with to develop the ideas within these pages. Thanks also to all the young writers who have agreed to let me publish their work even though I pay less than the *New Yorker.*

I am grateful to Claire Leach for reading an earlier version of the manuscript and giving some much-needed insight. I'm also indebted to Deborah Craig for her inspiring ideas and for sharing her wonderful class at Stratham Memorial school. Thanks also to Jennifer Luccah for setting us straight about why kids need to choose their own literature. Experiments with Anne Corrigan's fifth grade at Mary Hogan School, Peggy Tiffany's sixth—eighth grade at Halifax School, and Nancy Chaput's classes at Fairfield Center School were central in forming the ideas in this book. Thank you.

This book evolved out of work I did during the pilot year of Vermont's Portfolio Assessment project. Thanks to the teachers of Vermont, the Writing Leadership Committee, fellow Network Leaders, and Commissioner Richard Mills. Lynnda Buell of Advance Systems helped make the dream of portfolio assessment more of a reality. I am grateful for the outstanding work she did.

I'd like to especially thank Geof Hewitt for his wonderful ideas about revising poetry and Verandah Porche for teaching me word boxing.

Susan Wheeler's writing course remains a powerful influence on my ideas about writing, even though fifteen years have passed since I attended it! I am thankful to her and all my teachers and former colleagues at the University of New Hampshire, including the writing process founding fathers Donald Graves and Donald Murray. Collaborator and friend Bruce Ballenger's thoughts on research writing also helped shape certain chapters of the book. I delight in our continuing dialogue on the teaching of writing.

This book is dedicated to the memory of novelist and teacher Thomas Williams, who cared more about what language could say than anyone I have ever known.

Finally, I am grateful to my wife, Carol-Lee, for her patience, love, and laser-sharp editing skills; and my daughter Jessie Lynn for constantly teaching me that stories don't have to end—especially late at night when it's past her bedtime.

Shedding the Teacher Skin

I'm rewriting it while I'm writing it. It's changing itself.
Max Apple

I phoned Heinemann. My editor and friend Dawn Boyer liked the manuscript. She said it was great reading material, especially chapter 10 where I tear into basal readers. She said she laughed till she cried in her office.

It took a little courage for me to ask, but I finally did. "The introduction is a little weak, isn't it?" I asked in passing. "It is weak," she said. "It needs more."

I had already written it five times. It had seven different titles. From "Digging Potatoes" to "Re-shuffling Writing Process" to "Writing Process Revisited" to "Writing IS Revision," which until recently was the title of this book.

"You could make it a rationale for the book," Dawn went on to say. "You might want to give readers an idea of how the book is structured and why. A lot of writers write it the very last thing."

"OK," I said. "Sure I need to tell them how to use the book. Simple." I was talking to myself, the way writers do when they are trying to convince themselves of something they should know.

All the versions are still on the computer and I'm sitting here with a pen and paper trying to recreate an idea I had several hours ago when I was out running. I passed a house with two barking hounds on short leads. The dogs kept lunging at me, and as they did the collars tightened around their necks and jerked them back. It hit me that these dogs were modeling my own writing process. I'd start by barking, then lunge in a direction until something yanked me back. The problem with writing this introduction was that my line was too short and my collar too tight. I needed to cut myself some slack, and at that moment I realized that the best way to introduce this book on revision was simply to describe my struggle to write this introduction.

Teaching the constant struggle of the writer to find and shape meaning on the page is at the core of this book. I began writing it when I found that students, even in schools where writing process had been taught for ten years, wrote THE END in big letters at the end of each draft and rarely revised their work. Even teachers in these schools viewed revision as simply making a "sloppy copy" picture-perfect instead of as a means for discovery. Nothing new came after THE END.

My first introduction began with the question most asked by teachers at my in-service training workshops: "I can get them to write, but how do I get them to revise?" The question always disturbs me because it implies that a teacher must coerce a child into revision, whereas writing comes naturally. In that introduction

I talked about how writing-process theory unwittingly promoted this idea with a seven-step model that made revision one of the steps.

1. Brainstorm
2. Map
3. Freewrite
4. Draft
5. Revise
6. Clarify
7. Edit

I joked that my seven-step writing process looked more like this:

1. Revise
2. Revise
3. Revise
4. Revise
5. Revise
6. Revise
7. Revise

That was an OK lead but I felt that I was sermonizing, a bad habit. I also felt uncomfortable with the notion that my work is in conflict with writing-process theory when in reality it is simply creating a different model that will give students a more realistic, flexible view of revision to meet the needs of their own personal writing process. Before the book was accepted for publication one reviewer wrote, "Mr. Lane seems particularly obsessed with one stage of the writing process." I got all huffy because this reviewer clearly refused to accept that I was creating a new model for revision. "Since when was The Writing Process written on stone tablets?" I wrote to my editor.

Then I started thinking that anyone who writes a book for teachers, especially a practical one like this one, runs the risk of it being read as though it were written in stone, as a manual to be followed word for word—textbook fundamentalism I called it in that revision. I imagine that Donald Graves still cringes when he hears teachers talk of the Graves four-step writing process, and I was warned in another pre-acceptance review that some "unenlightened" teachers might grade students on how well they do my exercises. I started another introduction that highlighted the fact that all successful writing-process instruction depends on empowering students as writers, not simply following a prescribed formula.

This one began recounting a true story of a teacher at a training workshop who didn't want to be there. She corrected worksheets through my short lecture and was the first to tell me she had incorrectly done the writing exercise I'd given. When I told her it was OK, and that in fact an important part of a writer's development is to choose his or her own path, she became indignant and said, "If I give my students an assignment I expect them to do it!" Then she walked out of the meeting. At this point in that draft of the introduction I climbed back up on my soapbox and talked about how this book will be of little use if the reader takes the attitude of this teacher. Until a teacher promotes choice and responsibility among her students, the tools of craft this book has to offer won't help students to become writers. This book is not a recipe for revision that a teacher can prescribe. It's also not full of theory and brand-new scholarly research. Rather, it's a book of good ideas to help enrich and give versatility to the choices students make in their own writing.

This revision seemed awfully negative and even a little haughty. I am a writer who loves to teach writing, not some high-and-mighty authority. I am not a researcher in the scientific sense. My strength as a writer and a teacher come through what I have observed in my own work and the work of a wide range of teachers and students. If writing process has become institutionalized, I hope this book will help deinstitutionalize it. I want *all* teachers to read this book, not just teachers who are using writing process and have had success with collaborative learning. I want to convince teachers that these methods work, not condemn them for not making changes in their curriculums.

At this point I got very confused. I wandered aimlessly, reading books by Nancie Atwell, Donald Graves, Lucy Calkins, Frank Smith. I even lapsed into despair, wondering how important this book could be if I couldn't even write an introduction for it. At the same time I was finishing the book. When people asked me about it I'd say a little queasily, "It's a book on revision for teachers. It teaches a language of craft in short mini-lessons." (I threw in the writing-process lingo to make it sound as if I had it under control.)

The last week before the deadline I was asked to serve as a consultant at portfolio assessment meetings around the state of Vermont. I lugged my fifty pounds of computer to hotels, pecking away late into the night and early into the morning. One morning I arrived a little late at the meeting and found that my colleagues had been joking about my book. They said it would be the first book on revision to be published as a first draft. I laughed and quickly responded, "I do most of that revision stuff in my head anyway."

It hit me at that moment that this was a central part of the book: even a first draft is a revision of all the words I have yet to write. I wrote an ending that I really liked. Here it is:

From my work as a writer I know that revision is more than a stage in a four- five- or seven-step process; it is the source of the entire process. The moment I begin to write about my uncle, the moment I write the first sentence, "My uncle died when I was eight but nobody told me until I was twelve," I am beginning to revise the unwritten invisible text about my uncle. Why didn't I start with the stories my father told about him or about the black-and-white photo of him that hangs on my parents' wall? Why didn't I simply describe sitting on his lap as a child of two? Each word I write revises a hundred others I could have written, and when I go back to change passages I am always looking to measure what's there on the page against the wealth of unwritten material floating in my mind. Writing itself is revision, and if we can teach this concept to children and give them tools to develop it, they will experience the joy of discovery that keeps professional writers at their desks.

After THE END is packed with practical techniques to develop this sense of discovery for teachers and students alike. The book is geared to teachers of the upper elementary and middle grades through high school and into college and beyond, and it is divided into two parts: "Creating a Language of Craft" and "The Writer's Struggle." The former gives specific techniques to use in the classroom and to empower students with a language of craft; the latter helps teachers to identify and teach to the individual revising needs of their students. Each chapter is designed around several central "exercises" that teach concepts of craft such as details, leads, snapshots, "thoughtshots," scenes, and the like. The "exercise" is a tool for teaching—not an end in itself. Unlike ditto exercises, these exercises are meant to expand possibilities, get students thinking in ways they might not otherwise. Ideally, students will be able to apply these concepts to their own writing on their own chosen topics. Furthermore, if a student revises one of the exercises, please remember that that student is on the road to being a writer. And I encourage you to expand on these exercises to create your own.

To promote and encourage even more variation I have devised a series of supplementary exercises called spin-offs. These could be used as an alternative to the central exercise or as follow-up activities.

The chapters of the book build on each other but do not have to be read consecutively. I've designed the book so that the hurried teacher looking for a quick mini-lesson on voice can turn to chapter 11 and find some good ideas. If you're interested in reading in depth about the theory that underlies these ideas, I encourage you to read the wealth of material published. At the end of this book, I've included an annotated bibliography of the titles I've enjoyed learning from and that you might enjoy as well.

Some teachers may be puzzled that throughout the book I have made little mention of genre. This was intentional. Though I have tried to give examples of how the concepts of craft relate to research writing, science fiction, poetry, and nonfiction, to name a few, my hope is that by not limiting these concepts to specific genres, teachers and students will be encouraged to experiment with those concepts in the genres of their choice.

Finally, the goal of this book is to create a language of craft to share with your students. Though each writer's process is different, a shared language helps writers and readers to gain control. If writing, like carpentry, is a craft, then this book is a box of tools. Give your students the freedom to make choices of which tools to use when. Don't force students to use a screwdriver to hammer in a nail just because you think they need screwdriver practice. Point out possibilities and let *them* take action!

Traditionally, teachers have modeled perfection and students have struggled to meet that teacher's standards. Today, as teachers move toward individualized instruction and collaborative learning, students struggle to create and meet their own standards of excellence; teachers are learning to model the struggle. To illustrate this model I have included teachers' writing alongside students' writing throughout *After THE END*. Yet in talking about struggle it's also important to mention that we need to have *fun*. Writing *is* enjoyable. So is teaching. We can't take ourselves or the process too seriously or we risk losing all that we're starting to gain in education.

We need to laugh, to play around, to not be afraid of creating a mess or saying something wrong.

Ironically, though I wrote this book to help you model the struggle for your students, it took me six drafts of introduction before I was brave enough to model my own struggle for you. It's not easy to shed our expert/corrector teacher skin, but once we take the risk the dark, unreasonable, humorless clouds of perfection and expectation start to lift from our minds, and we join the ranks of the living, laughing, and learning. I hope this book will help you and your students take the risks that keep writers wanting to be at their desks long after THE END.

Creating a Language of Craft

> Books aren't written. They are rewritten.
>
> Michael Crichton

Good Writing Is Good Questions

Turning Questions into Leads

Questions are more important than answers. I'm looking for openings, not closings.
Madeline L'Engle

This was an exceptional fourth-grade class; college town; high salaries; low student ratios; first-rate music program; gifted and talented program. I had come to do a few writing workshops, to introduce a few new approaches to revision, and to explore the power of detail. Whole language and writing process were not new to this school.

I began to teach the students how to do web charts, but as soon as I made the first few circles on the flip chart I could hear groans and sighs. "Can't we just write?" a little girl in the front row asked. "Do we have to do that?" a freckle-face boy asked, raising his arms in frustration.

They had already learned web-charting; they had learned brainstorming; they had learned freewriting. These were the first three steps of the Vermont writing process, and they'd been told you had to do them in order. I did some serious backtracking. No, you didn't have to web-chart. It was just one tool in your writer's tool box, and so were brainstorming and freewriting. These were techniques to help you explore ideas. But if you wanted to you could just write. The students seemed relieved.

When I taught writing in the renowned process-writing composition program at the University of New Hampshire, my colleagues often remarked how wonderful it would be to teach students who had been taught the writing process since first grade. Concepts like finding your personal voice and the joy of freewriting would have been already taught. Students would already be fluent writers. How much farther we could take them! I was fortunate to have one such a student at UNH. He had gone to Oyster River School in Durham, New Hampshire, and had learned to freewrite in the first grade. He wrote with a strong personal voice and with great detail; but he had virtually nothing to say and had serious trouble revising any of his work. He wrote stifling essays about trips to the beach or going to parties. But it wasn't simply the subjects he chose; his lack of personal investment or enthusiasm about his message was the most disturbing element.

He was a charming student who wanted to please me, yet whenever I suggested revision for a deeper meaning during one of our weekly conferences he would say in a sleepy voice, "Maybe I should just freewrite a little more about that." I was at a loss. I wanted to grab him by the shoulders and shake some life into him and his writing. I wanted to shout, "It all counts!" but how could you teach that?

I suddenly began to appreciate the students who knew nothing at all about writing process until coming to UNH, students who had dribbled off five-paragraph themes their whole lives and now, suddenly, the floodgates were opening and their personal experiences were exploding on the page. I began to realize that to teach writing teachers must continually find new ways of revising their teaching, so that they teach an enthusiasm for innovation and constant revision that all writers share along with the ideas.

When I returned to that fourth-grade class two weeks later I decided I would not teach techniques of the writing process. Instead, I would find as many ways as I could to teach them the one thing all real writers had woven into their stories and essays and poems and books. I would teach them the one concept that fueled all writing processes. I would teach them that writing *is* revision. Here is what I did:

Growing Leads

1. "I have a really important story to tell you." I stood in front of the class. It was nine o'clock. "It's a scary story too. This is it. It happened when I was little and it was the most scared I had ever been in my life. There was this dog. And then my mother came and she rescued me. That's it." Silence. "Any questions?"

The hands dart into the air.
"What were you scared of?"
"What kind of dog?"
"What was his name?"
"Did the dog bite you?"
"What did the dog do?"
"How old were you?"
"What did your mother do to save you?"

2. I write their questions down as quickly as I can and list them on the board. I write fast because I want to model not losing your train of thought. I want to teach them how to jot things down before they float away.

3. By now they are dying to hear the story. I explain to them that every story begins by answering a question and some of their questions make me want to write more than others.

4. I answer each question with a complete sentence and turn it into a lead. For example, What kind of a dog was he and what was he doing? becomes "He was a big black dog and he was breathing down my neck."

5. Now that I have modeled the exercise the students pair up and tell each other about times they were scared. While the story is being told the listener thinks of five questions to ask and writes them down. Then they hand the questions to the teller. (Note: this can be done in groups of three to six. This way the storyteller gets more questions to choose from.)

6. I tell students each question is a string attached to their pens and they should pick two that tug the most and turn them into leads.

7. Have students pick their favorite lead, the one that makes them want to write the most, and then have them continue freewriting for ten to twenty minutes.

The stories are about being chased by older brothers, Halloween movies, the dark corner in the cellar. The questions point the writer in different directions, give the writer a new place to stand when he or she begins writing. Each lead is like the seed of a new revision. I tell them that all writing is a horse race of meaning. You have all this information and the more you revise the more certain horses keep taking the lead. Writing can be seen as answers to a series of questions. When the writer stops asking questions the horse race ends. The piece is over.

Look at this passage from a John McPhee essay on oranges and turn some of the sentences into questions.

The custom of drinking orange juice for breakfast is not very widespread, taking the world as a whole, and it is thought by many peoples to be a distinctly American habit. But many Danes drink it regularly with breakfast, and so do Hondurans, Filipinos, Jamaicans, and the wealthier citizens of Trinidad and Tobago. The day is started with orange juice in the Columbian Andes, and, to some extent, in Kuwait. Bolivians don't touch it at breakfast time, but they drink it steadily for the rest of the day. The "play lunch," or morning tea that Australian children carry with them to school is usually an orange, peeled spirally half down, with the peel replaced around the fruit. The child unwinds the peel and holds it as if it were an ice cream pop. People in Nepal never peel oranges, preferring to eat them cut in quarters, the way American athletes do. The sour oranges of Afghanistan customarily appear as seasoning agents on Afghan dinner tables. (p. 34)

Notice how McPhee, in *Oranges,* allows his curiosity to wander through the impressive research he has done. Like a young child his questions seem boundless, each answer spawning four or five more questions.

Unfortunately, I was never taught to ask questions in school and neither were most of the college freshmen who enter my classes. They were taught to write answers, to be experts, to lie. Questions were a threat to their knowledge. Questions were something that came numbered at the ends of chapters. Something that teachers asked. Something to ignore.

I tell students that good writing is fueled by unanswerable questions. Once they discover the joy every three-year-old and Ted Koppel knows, a world of knowledge is suddenly unlocked.

Several months later I tried this same exercise with a group of adult literacy tutors at a large conference where I gave a workshop. By now my exercise was called "the Navaho story circle meets Ted Koppel." I had read somewhere about the Navaho talking stick, which gives the power of total attention to the speaker. I use Bic pens, but this little prop gives an unexplainable power to the exercise. In my group a young woman writes about sitting in the back seat of her parents' car as it drifts from curb to curb. Her mother and father are both stone drunk and they have picked her up at the babysitter's. The more her mother complains about her husband's driving, the worse he drives. The young girl is petrified and furious with her mother for provoking him.

I write my questions.
- How old were you?
- How did you survive your childhood?
- How does anybody?

She likes the last two best and revises one into a lead. Later she tells me she has never written about these events before and she wonders if this is the reason she is bored with most of her writing. Could it be that these painful secrets stop her from writing anything meaningful? It is one of those questions that contains its own answer, so I simply ask her, "What do you think?"

The art of asking questions is intrinsically linked with the art of having something to say, of valuing your experience, and trusting enough to share even painful experiences, first with yourself and then with others.

When I teach writing I teach discovery. Techniques such as freewriting, brainstorming, and webbing are meaningless if we don't continue to find ways to tune students' ears to the surprises that await them. When I think of writing I think of a potato plant. Most of our writing is simply the leaves and stem of the plant, but as we revise more and more we dig for the right potato. A large part of writing is simply trusting your own instincts and asking questions that will help you dig deep enough.

Recently, a student in my freshman composition class wrote an essay about the difference between New Jersey and Vermont. The first few pages were what my colleagues cynically refer to as a see-saw essay. It had lines like New Jersey has pavement, Vermont has trees; New Jersey is frantic, Vermont is peaceful. But on page three a meaning began to emerge with the lines: "New Jersey is my father; Vermont is my mother. They've been divorced for ten years." He went on to describe how his mother was peaceful and his father was nervous and never satisfied. His mother was like him but his brother was like his father. Suddenly he was not describing landscapes but the most important relationships in his life. He had found his potato.

When the paper went before a writing workshop it was easy to find where the reader's interests lay. "When did your parents get divorced? Do they still live in New Jersey? Why did your mother move to Vermont?" Our instincts point us to meaning. We are all investigative journalists at heart, and questions are the fuel for all powerful writing.

The first step in learning that writing is revision is to learn to trust our instincts—to be three-year-old children once again. This metaphor springs to mind because I have been babysitting my three-year-old niece recently. I steal to the cupboard and discreetly sneak a piece of Halloween candy. I hear a voice call from the next room, "What you got? What you got your mouth?" Not wanting to lie but at the same time not wanting to model eating a Reeses Peanut Butter Cup for breakfast I say, "Oh nothing." She stares at me a moment with her big blue eyes and says, "I want some." Being the adult, I say, "You can't have candy for breakfast." She responds like the greatest of writers: "Why?"

Spinoffs

Try this question conference with stories your students have written.

• When a student reads a story out loud, ask the class to respond with questions about what they want to know more about. Make this a habit. Write the questions on the blackboard. Ask the writers to record the questions that intrigue them and make them want to write more. Teach them to notice that hungry feeling professional writers talk about when they find a question that makes them want to write more.

• Teach students to replace THE END with a list of five questions generated by a neighbor. Turn the best question into a new lead and try following it on another page.

• Circle one potential lead in a freewrite. Teach yourself this question: "If I began here where would I end up?"

• Read students leads from published books and then ask them to turn the leads into questions.

Seed Sentences: Leads and Research Papers

The most important sentence in a good book is the first one: it will contain the organic seed from which all that follows will grow.

Paul Horgan

Many writers remark about what could be called the Magic Line phenomenon. If they can find the right first sentence, the right lead, the piece will write itself. Some writers like John McPhee go as far as saying writing the lead is 90 percent of the work. McPhee calls leads magic flashlights that shine down through a piece of writing illuminating the way. Joan Didion says, "What's so hard about that first sentence is that you are stuck with it. Everything else is going to flow out of that sentence. And by the time you've laid down the first two sentences, your options are all gone" (Murray 1990, 12). Leads are not introductions writers nail on at the beginning of their pieces; they are seeds writers plant. Because different plants grow from different seeds, writers must search for the right lead.

Strong leads often leave questions in the reader's mind. Questions that make that reader want to read on. Look at how Russell Freedman introduces a chapter in his book *Indian Chiefs.*

They rode out of nowhere in quick attacks, stampeding horses and killing sentries with silent arrows. Then they vanished into the tall grass as quickly as they had come. (53)

Here's a few questions I have:

- Who is they?
- Where did they ride from? Where did they ride to?

In the next sentences Freedman begins to satisfy some of my curiosity.

Time and again during the early 1870's, Comanche warriors struck at the army's blue-coated cavalry troops, then lost themselves in the Texas Panhandle. The raiders were led by a young man riding a coal-black racing pony. His face was smeared with black war paint. His black hair hung in two braids like ropes over his shoulders. And his eyes were grayish-blue. The Commanches called him Quanah. The Texans knew him as the notorious half-breed war chief, Quanah Parker. (53)

All we have to do is imagine an encyclopedia entry on Quanah Parker to understand the importance of strong leads.

Quanah Parker was born in . . .

Which piece would you rather read? Which would you rather write? Freedman, a skilled journalist, knows that to interest readers he must engage their curiosity. He doles out information in dribs and drabs, coloring and pacing his story like an expert filmmaker. A skilled magazine writer can make *any* subject fascinating, yet in school we teach children to write research papers that often end up being lists of facts nailed together instead of a legitimate inquiry into a topic.

Recently, a teacher was puzzled by the portfolio assessment criteria that forced him to evaluate the qualities of distinctive voice or effective tone in a research paper. "Is my goal as a teacher to get my students to entertain me?" he asked. I told him the goal was to get the next generation of *Scientific American* writers to write more like the writers of *National Geographic*. Writers like Stephen Jay Gould and Carl Sagan have proven that even the most complex ideas can be made fun to read when the author lets some of his or her own personal curiosity leak through the page.

Finding leads through this questioning process, or just writing the lead first and asking the questions second, is an excellent way to get a distinctive voice or effective tone into a research paper and eventually, after determining what the best questions are, to formulate a thesis. My friend Bruce Ballenger taught me how to teach curiosity about research topics when we shared an office as graduate students at the University of New Hampshire. Bruce created question galleries in his classroom in order to let students' natural interest be the driving force in their research.

Finding the Heart of the Research

1. Students write their ten best questions on large sheets of newsprint (endrolls that most newspapers still give away).

2. Sheets of questions are tacked up around the classroom with masking tape, creating a question gallery.

3. Students read one another's questions, checking off ones they are most interested in and writing one new question at the bottom of the list.

4. After sharing all the lists of questions with the whole class, students then return to their own questions, taking note of the class's intrigue and the new questions that grew out of it. Students pick several questions and begin researching. Once they've found some interesting information, they formulate a new list of more specific questions.

5. Repeat the process. This time, the questions will be more focused and more deeply rooted in the students' inquiry. Explain to students that researchers are detectives searching for clues that take them deeper and deeper into the mystery.

6. Teach students to write a statement based on the most interesting research they have found.

A thesis is in essence a good lead, a seed from which all of the research grows. The same applies for the personal research I might do in libraries when writing a personal narrative about my grandmother. Leads are probably the best revising tool a writer has. Pillage the bookshelves in your school library and find strong leads. Read the leads to your class and ask students to think about questions they have. Teach students to listen to the invisible questions that whisper in readers' ears, begging them to read on.

Spinoffs

- Find examples of good scientific writing and read them to the class. Discuss what qualities in the writing make it interesting to the reader. Then find a short but very boring piece of scientific writing. Break the class into small groups and ask them to rewrite the lead or the entire piece to make it interesting. Suggest that they begin by listing questions to find a compelling lead.

- To encourage the habit of asking questions, create question conferences on a regular basis where students read each other's papers and ask each other probing questions on paper. Tell students that it's not important to answer every question, rather to find those questions that make them want to write more—to pursue new leads or information to be inserted into their stories.

- Encourage students when studying any subject to make long lists of questions. You can do this with them or they can do it in small groups. Illustrate how one question sparks another. Fill the walls of your classroom with questions and practice asking them every day. Before long you will have a class of active listeners, and students will begin thinking more and more like revising writers.

- Make a Question Box and put it somewhere in the classroom. Encourage students to put questions anonymously in the box. Every once in a while read the questions to the class to spark a discussion.

- Have students start a list of unanswerable questions in their journal and add to it throughout the year. Suggest they try answering one on a day when they're at a loss for a topic.

More than Wallpaper

Using Details to Develop Focus and Meaning

Prose is architecture not interior decoration.
Ernest Hemingway

"If I were to tell you that the maple tree outside there on the playground just said to itself, 'I'm sick of being a tree. I think I want to be a person now,' and if I told you that maple tree got up and is now sprinting down Interstate 89, what would you say?"

The students pause a minute, then sigh, then groan. "No way! Trees don't run."

"OK, OK. But what if I said, 'The maple tree decided it didn't want to be a tree anymore and is running down Route 89 and there is a little boy named Seth chasing after it and a blue Chevy Cavalier wagon. And it just stepped on my 1979 Toyota Liftback, crushing the box of Twix candy bars I was saving to bring to class tomorrow.' What if I were to say, 'There is a cat up in the tree, and the fire department is chasing after it, and that cat is howling like a wolf on the highest branch, and the principal, Mrs. Stewart, has lassoed it with an orange extension cord and tied it to the bumper of school bus number ten.' If I could tell you enough details, so that you actually started to see this runaway tree, if I could make you begin to imagine something exact and real about this runaway tree, you might, you just might, go to the window and look. That's what writers do. They make you go to the window and look."

This is how I introduce students to the concept of detail, the best tool any writer has to bring writing into focus and find deeper meaning. I begin this way because I want them to see right from the start that details are not ends in themselves but always serve to bring to life some larger vision of the writer. This was something I never learned in school. I learned to fill pages with adjectives that only padded the story and did little to forward my purpose. But how do we teach students to discriminate between the purposeful and the extraneous? How do we teach them that details are not wallpaper but walls?

Recently, my mother gave me a floppy, black leather winter hat. It's one of those old ones, with puppy-dog earflaps and silver snaps that convert it into a Russian-style hat. It had been sitting in a damp cellar for years, and she thrust it at me as I prepared to leave one evening and said, "Here, you need this, it's cold in Vermont." You have to know my mother to understand this. The hat was too tight, it made me look geek-like, and to top it off, it smelled like sweaty socks. I vaguely remember my father wearing it some twenty years ago. It was only by coincidence that it happened to be in my travel bag the next day when I was doing a workshop with some eighth graders.

I used to use a rock or a piece of chalk for this exercise, but now I take this hat wherever I go. Here's how it works.

Digging for Details

1. After describing to students that writers make things come alive (my running tree story or your own equivalent) I take out this smelly old hat. (I suppose any slightly unusual garment would work, but hats are particularly funny by nature.) I tell the students that the more we describe this hat the more it will come alive. I have them pass it around the class and say the first thing that comes into their heads about the hat, using their five senses as a guide. I write their details quickly on the board.

2. I read through their details, which are usually fairly general like "black," "smells weird," "fuzzy," and then I tell them that the hat is beginning to come awake after sleeping in my mother's cellar.

3. I describe to the students how the more writers struggle to describe something the more it comes alive. I give them an example of a woman on a bus who was trying to tell me what building she worked in. First she said, "It's the tall one." I asked her, "Could you be a little more specific?" and I talk briefly with the class about what that word means. Then she said, "It's the fourth one in," and I still didn't know what she meant. But finally, after she stopped and thought for a minute, she said, "It's that funny-looking one standing on four legs with the dark Chiclet-shaped windows that make it look like an air-traffic control tower." I talk about how it wasn't her first detail that made her description come alive. It took a bit of digging on her part. Now we are going to dig for *specific* details.

4. I ask for a volunteer. I put the funny hat on the volunteer's head and tell the class, "Michelle has just walked into your story. Do you say, 'She was wearing a black hat?' "

"No," they reply.

"OK, now let's *really* describe this hat."

There is usually a slight hesitation, and then they start in.

If they don't, I play with the flaps of the hat or ask them, "What's it look like?"

"A motorcycle helmet."

"An exploding basketball."

"A pilot's hat."

"Looks weird."

"Why's it look weird?" I ask.

"Looks like General Eisenhower."

I fill the board with these fresher ideas, and if we get stuck I go back to our first list and take details like "smells weird" and ask Why? or How? Answers like "smells like my dog," add to the list of specific details.

5. Next, I build a description using their best details. You can do this aloud or on the board. You could even try having the students write the description. "He was wearing a black fuzzy hat that was weird. It had big puppy-dog flaps that made him look like Dumbo ready to take off or General Eisenhower on a bad day. It was as if a basketball had exploded on his head, and when he walked by me I almost choked on the moldy smell of dirty socks."

6. I ask students, "Which list of details was more fun to make?" They always say the second, when they described the hat on their classmate's head. I remind them how difficult it was for them to come up with details the first time but the second time I had to stop because I ran out of board space. "That's why writers love to write," I say. "They discover things. They surprise themselves the more they dig deeper into a subject. But it doesn't happen at first—it takes practice to develop new habits of seeing, to turn the knob on the binoculars in order to go beyond a blurry lead like, 'I walked into the classroom. There were a bunch of desks and a bunch of kids' to 'A teenage boy sat in the front row with his hands stuck inside the chipped formica desk that was inscribed with the logos of most major heavy metal bands. He wore a black Metallica tee-shirt with cigarette burn craters that exposed his pale skin.'

Now that students have had practice digging for details it's time to apply the skill to their own writing.

A Room with a View

1. Have students close their eyes and think of a room they know well. Ask them to think of all the details in that room. Remember, a detail can be anything in that room, even how that room smells or a memory of a mother sitting in a chair.

2. Ask them to open their eyes and write down five quick details about the room.

3. Have them find a partner and take turns asking each other questions about each detail to make it more specific. Write down the specific details next to the original.

Example: My mother sitting in a chair.
My mother sitting in the rocking chair knitting a pink sweater for my Aunt Margaret's latest brat.

4. (optional). Have students freewrite starting with a sentence that includes their favorite detail. Ask them, "Where did that detail lead you?"

I end this exercise by challenging students to stop, think, and ask themselves questions whenever they get stuck trying to describe something. Add that extra specific detail, that phrase or two that makes it all come alive. Turn the knob on the binoculars for a sharper focus. Your room can be messy but readers won't really know it till they see the shirts and blouses wrestling with each other on the tan carpet, till they smell the aroma of old socks and hear the overhead fan whining with the weight of wet blue jeans that spin round and round like a pair of legs trying to dance with their shadow.

This exercise takes about ten to fifteen minutes and is a good lead-in to the next one, where we dig deeper for fictional details.

Digging for Fictional Details

1. Write on the board "He/she liked crazy clothes," or my current favorite for fourth through eighth grade: "It was a much more awesome planet for kids than earth." Or have your students make up several of their own sentences. Tell the students that they need to make the sentence come alive with specific details or the reader won't even begin to believe them. The questioning process is the same for fiction as for nonfiction writing. To begin, ask students to quickly list fifteen details of their planet or crazy clothes or whatever sentence on the board interests them. Remind them that they don't have to labor over this list.

2. When they're done with their initial list ask them to find a partner to help them dig for more specific details. Repeat the same process as in the last exercise. Each person alternately reads one detail off their list and the other person asks them three or four questions to help the partner get more specific. The writer then writes down the more specific details. (This exercise also works well with small groups. Simply have each group member ask a question or two for each detail and take turns writing down the more specific details.)

Example: There are no parents on the planet.

> Where do kids come from?
> They spew out of volcanoes once a year.
> But where do they get born?
> They don't get born; they were created at the begining of time, like rocks.

Example: *jeans*

> What color?
>> Pink with green polka dots.
> What condition?
>> Big tears at each knee and a faded Russian flag sewn into crotch.

Remind students that questions that begin with "What" are usually more helpful than the "yes or no" questions that begin with "Is." Model this questioning process a few times with the group and then let the students go at it.

3. (optional). Ask students to draw a picture of their person or planet including all their detail. If they end up drawing more than they wrote about, have them add extra details to their written list.

4. Have students share their details (and drawings) with the rest of the class. Talk about which details stand out the most and why. Ask students to explain how their details altered from the first list to the second.

Problem People/Problem Planets

After students have a list of details about their subject, ask them this one question: What's the problem? Every subject must have a problem or else it is uninteresting. Have the students who want to write a story about their subject and the problem.

"But my planet's more awesome than Earth. There are no problems," the student says. One reply is, "Your problem can be that you have no problems. How does that affect people on your planet? How would it affect a visitor from Earth? Every planet has a problem."

Teachers often complain to me about the lack of detail and the formulaic quality in the science fiction or fantasy stories their students write. I tell them that students need to learn the need to make fantasy stories come alive, and we can teach them by showing them how enjoyable it is to dig deeper and discover more about even the most bizarre worlds. Once they know this process through nonfiction writing, it's easy to illustrate how it can bring fiction writing to life.

Though fantasy writing is in some ways more demanding because students are called on to use their imaginations instead of their memories to find details, once writers develop the habit of questioning to find more specific details imaginations usually meet the challenge. Outlawing fantasy in your classroom is not the answer, especially if it inspires some writers. It's better to teach students the need to make fantasy real and give them the tools to do so.

Building Character

As students develop a concept of detail it can help them to dig deeper into the characters they create. Detail and character development go hand in hand. I begin the following exercise by telling students that many novelists like Robert Newton Peck or Joyce Carol Oates write pages of notes about a character before they put him or her into a story. Though they don't always use all the information they unearth through digging for details, knowing their characters better helps them to write the story.

1. Have students make a list of ten details of a character they want to create.

2. Ask students to give the character a problem.

3. Have students stand in front of the class and become the character. They can introduce themselves to the class and tell the class about the problem. Then they can take questions.

4. Ask them to return to their seat and write down what they learned about their character.

5. Ask them to write a story with their character in it.

When many people walk into the dentist office, they sit down in a chair and find the nearest magazine. But when a writer walks in, she notices the bizarre-looking man with one eye sitting in the corner reading a *National Geographic* magazine. A writer sees the red patent leather chairs, the cream-colored textured wallpaper that gives the place that middle-class, rec room feeling. A writer sees that the fish tank is neglected, half-filled with algae, and that one of the goldfish is fatter and older than the rest, probably for some sinister reason. A writer hears the Burt Bacharach litanies reverberating just below the level of consciousness and perhaps even has a few theories about those raindrops that keep falling on your head. If you could cut open a writer's mind you would see questions. Growing one out of the other.

- What kind of room is it?
- Who's there? What do they look like? What are their lives like? What are they reading?
- What else is in the room? What's the fish tank look like?
- What kind of fish are in it?
- What kind of music is playing? What does it sound like?
- What does it remind you of?

Figure 2–1 Jeffrey's Story

MY GRAMMY

My grammy has around 40 grandchildren. Some are old. Some are young. She has around 4 boys and one girl. They're all grown up. She has a trailer in Northfield Falls and beside the trailer she has some boards shaped as a little house with yellow and tin on the roof. She has more than 1000 salt and pepper shakers. All of them are worth around $2,000,000. Grammy's real name is Bernice Drown. She has a big backyard that I play on and when Grammy mows it I rake it. Grammy's house is real crowded. She has two refrigerators and two stoves, two bedrooms and two bathrooms, one kitchen, one living room and a toy room. Grammy has a roof hitched to her trailer to cover her car. Almost every Saturday she goes to lawn sales and every Sunday she goes to church. I don't think she missed one day of church. She's the one that got me to go to church. My grammy has a blue station wagon with a nine inch stuffed pencil with eyes and a mouth. She hardly ever swears and really believes in Jesus. She doesn't like to waste a thing. When Grammy's at our house eating and we don't want a piece of food just say we're going to throw it away and she will eat it!

by Jeffrey Drown

Rich detail is the end result of an inquisitive mind. When we look at fourth grader Jeffrey Drown's sketch of his beloved grandmother shown in Figure 2–1, we see much more than an essay written for a teacher by a fourth grader. We see a mind searching for the right details to make Grammy come alive. We can teach students to look beyond first impressions to the wonderful afterthoughts that come with revision.

Spinoffs

- Have students swap stories and ask five questions that will add detail to a story.
- Ask students to circle their favorite details in a story they've written. Have them ask questions about something in the story and add at least three new details.
- Ask students to find a piece of fruit at home. Have them

cut it open and write about it for fifteen minutes engaging all their senses. Ask them to eat it and continue writing.

- Teach students to practice unsticking themselves. Have them describe something to the classroom. Ask them to write a sentence or two and stop. Have them ask a question silently to themselves, then continue writing with the answer. Discuss the power of questions to help writers see more.

- Send students outdoors with their notebooks. Ask them to write down fifteen details of the day and then come back to their classroom. At their desks ask them to write fifteen more details. Remind them to ask questions about their first list to find more detail.

- Divide the class into an even number of small groups. Pass out one artist postcard per small group. Ask students to describe their picture in exact physical detail, so that a blind person could imagine it. (Don't let any group see the other groups' cards.) After each group writes a description of their picture, take away all the postcards and ask the groups to exchange descriptions. Then ask each member of the group to draw the picture of the postcard based on the description. When the drawings are done, pass out the postcards and compare them to the drawings. Re-read the descriptions and talk about what language was effective and what led them astray.

- Ask students to generate a list of fifteen questions that might be asked upon entering a room, then take their list to a room and write fifteen more questions based on what is there. Have them re-read their list, answering five questions that make the most sense and turning them into a description of the room.

three

Snapshots and Thoughtshots

Writing is not writing skills, but knowing how to see.... There are people who can't read or write who are novelists. They've got two lenses. A telephoto lens for big pictures and a lens a dentist would use. What they do to show the big picture is to use details they see with the small lens.

Carolyn Chute

Snapshots

"How many of you just LOVE revising?" There is a noticeable groan. Two or three hands go up but the majority scowls. When I ask them why they hate it they say, "When I write something once I don't like to write it over." "I hate rewriting." Most, if not all, of students' dislike and distress about revision involves revising what is on the page, not what hasn't been written yet. This is normal; no one likes to rewrite, copy over what they have already written. But that isn't revision.

Consider for a moment the writer struggling to find a lead into his or her subject. I wrote this a few minutes ago trying to start this chapter:

Now that we know how to find good leads and understand detail we are ready to explore techniques to teach revision of a particular subject. Today I will demonstrate how to trick students into revising their subjects before they think of themselves as writing a finished draft. But before I do, let's examine the life of a professional writer and see how it may apply to the classroom writer.

It said what I wanted it to but it seemed too dry, as if I were following some logical progression. I was sounding too much like an expert and that both scared and bored me. So I thought to myself, I want something that is closer to the classroom, and I wrote, " 'How many of you just love revising?' There was a noticeable groan."

I like this better because it's closer to the individual student, and I know from experience that teachers often hear the voices of students in their heads when they read books about teaching. But perhaps I should move even closer to an individual student and relate a real incident. Something like, " 'It's done!' Keith said. He stared at me with his big brown eyes as his lips tightened into a pronounced pout. His fists tightened and he thrust the piece of paper at me." Yes, I think I like this lead even better.

Writers are like photographers with giant zoom lenses, observing life in incredibly fine detail, pulling back to make sweeping generalizations, then zooming in again to make those generalizations come alive with detail, as we did in the last chapter.

I've developed a concept called "snapshot" to teach writers to write in sharp physical detail. Here is a snapshot of Ma putting the children to bed from *Laura Ingalls Wilder's Little House in the Big Woods* (1971).

Ma kissed them both, and tucked the covers in around them. They lay there awhile, looking at Ma's smooth, parted hair and her hands busy with sewing in the lamplight. Her needle made little clicking sounds against her thimble and then the thread went softly, swish! through the pretty calico that Pa had traded furs for.

Notice how Ingalls Wilder zooms in closer to her subject with more particular physical detail in each sentence. I sometimes tell students that details are boxes inside boxes. One detail unlocks several others, and so on. Laura Ingalls Wilder begins by looking at Ma and ends up dwelling on Ma's hands sewing. This telephoto quality becomes sharply apparent when we convert this snapshot back into the questions Laura Ingalls Wilder may have asked in her mind as she wrote this passage. Here's what I came up with.

- What did Ma do to put the girls to bed?
- What did the girls look at?
- What did Ma's hair look like? How was it parted?
- What were Ma's hands doing?
- How much light was in the room?
- What did the needle sound like when it hit against the thimble?
- What did the thread sound like when it went through the calico?
- Where did the calico come from?

Laura Ingalls Wilder's wonderful books are full of these moments where the smallest detail like a needle clicking against a thimble brings an entire world alive in the reader's mind. Making students aware of the thought processes of a master writer is a wonderful way to model craft for their own writing.

Another way is to simply read great literature often pointing out the qualities of craft we have discussed. When I read snapshots to students I usually ask them this question: "What detail sticks with you the most?" Think about this as you read the next snapshot of a baker from the short story, "A Small Good Thing" by Raymond Carver.

The baker, who was an older man with a thick neck, listened without saying anything when she told him the child would be eight years next Monday. The Baker wore a white apron that looked like a smock. Straps cut under his arms, went around back and then to the front again where they were secured under his heavy waist. He wiped his hands on his apron as he listened to her. He kept his eyes down on the photographs and let her talk. He let her take her time. He'd just come to work and he'd be there all night, baking, and he was in no real hurry. (1983)

For me it's the way he wipes his hands on his apron as he listens. I can see this big guy standing, smearing flour on his apron as he talks to her. This one detail makes the baker come alive for me. For you it might be the baker's thick neck or the way he doesn't look up from the photographs of birthday cakes as the woman talks to him. Like Laura Ingalls Wilder, Raymond Carver gives us many physical details about his subject and each detail brings a little more life and another chance for the reader to be drawn in. Look at the way Jerry Spinelli makes a dilapidated house come alive in his young adult novel *Maniac Magee:*

Maniac had seen some amazing things in his lifetime, but nothing as amazing as that house. From the smell of it, he knew this wasn't the first time an animal had relieved itself on the rugless floor. In fact, in another corner he spotted a form of relief that could not be soaked up by newspapers.

Cans and bottles lay all over, along with crusts, peelings, cores, scraps, rinds, wrappers—everything you would normally find in a garbage can. And everywhere there were raisins.

As he walked through the dining room, something—an old tennis ball—hit him on top of the head and bounced away. He looked up—into the laughing faces of Russell and Piper. The hole in the ceiling was so big they both could have jumped through it at once.

He ran a hand along one wall. The peeling paint came off like cornflakes.

Nothing could be worse than the living and dining rooms, yet the kitchen was. A jar of peanut butter had crashed to the floor; someone had gotten a running start, jumped into it, and skied a brown, one-footed track to the stove. On the table were what appeared to be the remains of an autopsy performed upon a large bird, possibly a crow. The refrigerator contained two food groups: mustard and beer. The raisins here were even more abundant. He spotted several of them moving. They weren't raisins; they were roaches. (1990, pp. 131–32)

Writers need to develop the habit of seeing the world in close physical detail. We began the last chapter by digging for details.

In this chapter, we will go deeper into different types of detail and the value of discerning the differences in the student's reading and writing.

Alisa Johnson is a sixth grader at Mallet's Bay School in Colchester, Vermont. Her snapshot of entering the house after a morning of sledding is packed with the same type of well-observed physical detail we've seen in the works of the masters:

I went inside. The smell of hot cocoa flowed throughout the house. The fire crackled in the small read and brown bricked fireplace. My mother was stirring the beef soup. My two year old brother was quietly playing with wooden blocks that had little letters carved in them. My father sat playing a slow, sad song on his beautiful country guitar. I took off my parka and hung it on the brass coatrack. My mother gave me a bowl of hot beef soup and cocoa. The broth felt warm running down my throat. The feeling of warmth spread all over me.

Alisa understands the power of physical detail to create a mood. She could have just written, "I went inside and it was warm and wonderful and everyone was there," but then we wouldn't see her brother playing quietly with his blocks or hear her father playing the slow sad song on his country guitar. We wouldn't smell the hot beef soup or the cocoa. We wouldn't feel the warm broth running down her throat. Learning to write in physical detail is often the process of slowing down our senses and truly observing the world around us. Building on the ability to dig for details, the following exercise teaches students to observe moments in *closer* physical detail.

The Magic Camera

1. Begin by explaining to students that writers have a magic camera that they can point at the world and create snapshots that contain smells and sounds as well as colors and light. Read several examples of snapshots from literature and discuss why a writer like Laura Ingalls Wilder doesn't just write, "Ma put the kids to bed and did some sewing till they fell asleep."

2. Review some of the things writers can do to dig deeper for details when they stall out. Make sure they remember the power of asking questions to dig up more "specific" detail.

3. Ask students to think of a person they know very well. Then ask them to place that person in the middle of an empty page and then pretend they have a magic camera that can freeze any moment in time since they've known that person. Web-chart at least five or six moments, briefly noting them.

4. Have students pick one moment and write a snapshot of that one moment. (Make sure it's only one moment that students write about.) Create a picture with words of that moment. For example, instead of "Dad took me ice fishing," we have "Dad knelt beside me by the ice hole, his hand in the icy water reaching for the perch that slipped back in."

5. Ask students to write for twenty minutes or however long it takes to create a snapshot of their person. When finished, students read over what they've written and ask themselves at least two questions that will lead to more detail. Then have them go back and either insert or add this detail to their snapshots.

6. Students share snapshots with a partner or group. The listeners write down questions that grow out of their natural curiosity about the person. The writer adds more detail to the original snapshot.

7. Have students draw a picture of their snapshot, putting in all the detail from their words. Students then add one or two more details from their drawing to their writing.

When I asked sixth grader Candace to write a few snapshots of her mother, her mind went blank. Her freewrite had begun, "My mother is the biggest influence on my life," and though full of passion, was stuck in the clouds of vague truth. Later, I was told by her teacher that this was a chronic problem in her writing. When I looked at her paper I saw only one sentence: "My mother is sitting by the fireplace." "What is she doing?" I asked. "Nothing," Candace replied in a shy, almost embarrassed voice. She was an eighth grader with curly blonde hair and inquisitive blue eyes. The bland quality of her writing seemed to contradict the spark in those eyes. "Nothing?" I asked. "Well, she's patting the dog. And she does other things too." "You could write about all of it," I suggested. That's all she needed to produce this snapshot.

She was sitting by the fire with her head down, looking at the dog. As she was looking she was petting the sleeping dog with a brown and shiny coat. The dog was regular size sitting next to her with the face of the dog on its side. She was being warmed by the warm fire in the olive and black stove. She was sitting indian style with her other hand on her lap holding a cigarette. She seemed to be thinking hard about something, something important to her. Maybe her children, maybe her dog. No one knows what.

Learning the concept of the "snapshot" gave Candace a tool for zooming in on her subject and seeing beyond her preconceived thoughts and feelings about her mother to an objective reality that was more mysterious and compelling for both the writer and the reader. My experience as a writing teacher in many classrooms tells me that most students who say they are bored with writing or revising are really just bored with their notion of writing. Revision becomes exciting the more options a writer has, but most inexperienced writers limit their options, and teachers sometimes encourage these limitations by rushing papers to completion so that students can be held accountable for grammar and punctuation. In chapters 14 and 15 of this book I'll show you new ways to teach grammar and punctuation without waiting for the final draft. When we understand that the writing process is not a list of steps to be followed in order, but a recursive journey, revision can become a mesmerizing activity.

Here's an exercise that builds on the last one. It teaches students how to zoom in with detail and pull back to reflect on new directions and possibilities before they've solidified their ideas into a draft.

Groping for a Start

This exercise can be done in an hour or spread out over several days. The order is not important. Try reshuffling the steps or add some of your own. The goal here is to give students a feeling for the many different places they can begin when writing about a subject.

1. Ask students to write another snapshot of their person from the last exercise.

2. Have students brainstorm a list of fifteen details about their person. A detail can be anything from "He is tall," to "He

hates pepperoni pizza." Students can then pick the best detail and turn it into a lead sentence.

3. Have students freewrite for ten minutes, either following their lead or one of their snapshots.

4. Students share their freewrites with partners or groups. Listeners write questions on scraps of paper and hand them to the writer. The writer picks the question that intrigues him or her the most and turns it into a lead by answering it. (See chapter 1—this may need to be modeled again.)

5. Students freewrite for ten minutes following this new lead.

6. Have students make a web chart of their person and turn the most interesting strand into a new lead.

7. Students read their snapshots and freewrites and circle two possible new leads.

8. By now students have seven distinct places to begin writing about their subject. Explain to students that each new lead, just like each new snapshot, is a revision. They don't have to wait till they finish a draft to revise. They can do it all the time.

9. Ask students to compare their different pieces. Have students pick the most compelling and write to the end of the period and longer if they want to.

When I presented this exercise to a group of elementary school teachers, one told me he really liked the process of standing back and turning questions to new leads. It taught him the writer's quest to find something new about his subject. He also felt the snapshots helped him to remember things he thought he had long since forgotten about his subject. But then he paused a moment and said, "I'm confused about how we move from this stage to a finished story."

"Most writers are confused about that too," I said. Actually that is what I would have liked to have said. In reality I tried to explain that there was no real formula for a finished story. Yes, I know for years teachers have been telling us about conflict, climax, denouement, resolutions, introductions, bodies, and conclusions, but in reality those teachers lied to us. Though stories and essays have some of these elements, and there is nothing inherently wrong with formula writing, the problem comes when we confuse forms with skills.

Real stories or essays are as complex and unique as the writers who struggle to make them. To assume, as many of my teachers did, that a successful writer should be able to produce a well-constructed essay of five paragraphs is to confuse a particular academic form with the skill of writing with meaning and purpose. As student-centered, process-oriented curriculums develop that don't require a writing assignment to be finished by the end of a day, we have begun to struggle with teaching craft as opposed to ready-made forms. As students wean themselves from formulas, their jobs become much more complex and multi-faceted. They become writers struggling to create form and meaning as they go. At this point *they* are free to choose a form or genre to explore as opposed to the form choosing them. In chapter 6 I'll show some new ways of getting a handle on this complexity, but for now think of this exercise as showing students a few places where they could begin writing. We are developing the writer's instinct to choose one place over another.

Consider Sarah, a speech pathologist writing about a childhood memory that flashed into her journal while doing the above exercise.

Next door I hear Tommy Fenton's father threatening to beat him if he doesn't do what he is supposed to. The overweight, flabby, greasy coal black haired father begins counting to 10. 1 . . . 2 . . . 3. . . . I see Tommy make a run for it, through the breezeway, out into the backyard, defying his father's warning. My sister and I don't play with Tommy but he is about our age. I just see him across our corn field. His hair sticks up on end and he's so skinny and wiry.

Later Sarah turned the question "Who was Tommy Fenton and what does he mean to you now?" into a lead.

Tommy Fenton was my neighbor on Webster Road in Orchard Park, New York. I thought that I had forgotten his name. How his name flew off my pen that morning I do not understand. I began writing without thinking. Back then I was too little to help Tommy but I have helped many children in many ways in the years since. For all I know his father was not an abuser. At the time I believed he was.

Whether Sarah can successfully combine this lead into an essay with a beginning, middle, and end is irrelevant at this point. It is much more important that she is learning the powers of craft that have allowed her to zoom in on moments and pull back to find out what they mean. These qualities are the backbone of all great literature and the glue that keeps writers sitting at their desks. Writers don't need to be given formulas; they need to be shown possibilities. Then, like painters receiving new colors, they can embrace their craft.

Spinoffs

- Take students through the steps of this exercise using a place instead of a person.
- Students take three or four snapshots of anything. They pick one snapshot, draw a picture of it, and write more about it.
- Students write a dialogue between two characters. After they've written it, they can go back and insert snapshots. Demonstrate the power of snapshots by reading a scene from a novel without snapshots and then reading it over including them.
- Have students write a snapshot, where they pretend to be their person writing about themselves. This self-portrait should reflect qualities that this person might see in the student. For example, when would their little brother choose to pull out his magic camera and point it at them?
- Students write several snapshots of their home town or any town.
- Collect several snapshots of characters from novels. Write several on the board and ask the class to draw a picture of the person of their choice. Remark on the power of detail to create images in the reader's mind.
- Ask for three volunteers. Assign one to be the character's thoughts, one to be his or her nose, and one to be his or her eyes. Ask the volunteers to put the character in a situation and have them call on their assigned senses to fill in specific detail.
- Ask students to read over a story they've written and find a place to insert a snapshot. Have them place a caret [^] mark in this spot in their story and write their snapshot on a sepa-

rate piece of paper. Following is an example from Heidi McMann's story:

Ben Hale was about to be hanged. For spying. They brought him out. I said, "Lord please forgive this man. And the men about to hang him. He was only doing something for his country that he thought was right. Amen." I stepped down. They kicked the ladder out from under him. In ten seconds he was dead. But it seemed like an eternity. [She places a caret (^) here; the snapshot she wants to insert appears below.] I went back into my quarters. There I splashed cold water on my face and prayed. Then I wrote a letter to my wife Marlin and my son John who is eighteen. I told them how I. . . .

[Heidi's snapshot:]

The man's hands were flopped strait [sic] down toward the ground. His chin was pressed against his chest. His face was blue, his eyes were still open. His legs were just dangling there. His mouth was pursed. His chest looked tough and mighty before but not much anymore.

The Mountain and the Sea

We write to taste life twice, in the moment, and in introspection."

Anaïs Nin

My model for the writing process is different from the list of stages I see in many classrooms. It's what I call "the mountain of perception and the sea of experience." (See Figure 3–1.) All writing begins in the sea of experience, with what we know. Our memories swim with disconnected but vivid sights and sounds and smells. When we write, we begin to climb the mountain and see the patterns beneath the water; we begin to make sense of our lives and revise what we write. But to make these abstract thoughts come to life, we need to return to the sea to gather all the details. As writers, we continually move back and forth between the sea and the mountain. Candace did this when she wrote her snapshot of her mother and we could see her sitting by the fireplace with the dog sleeping beside her.

Figure 3–1   The Mountain of Perception and the Sea of Experience

Great writing moves up and down the mountain, sometimes in the same sentence. Problems occur when the writer gets stuck in either occupation. A writer bogged down in the sea fills pages with meaningless detail about events or people that have nothing to do with their larger purpose. This "potatoless" prose can be remedied if the writer climbs the mountain a bit and gazes down on the patterns beneath. Consider a piece of writing that begins, "The sun was shining. The daffodils were blooming. The grass was green. It was a warm day." There is not much of a reason to write or read on. You could say that the writer was a little stuck in the sea of experience and would benefit by climbing. Here is a revision that climbs the mountain a little and gets closer to the potato of the story: "The day my grandmother died the sun was shining. The daffodils were blooming. The grass was green. It was a warm day." Notice how climbing the mountain creates a frame around details and suddenly they seem more pertinent.

However, climbing the mountain is not without its own hazards. You could get stuck up there in the clouds of general and Godlike truth, writing thoughts like, "VCRs: everybody has them," or "The United States is a great country." These writers need to come down out of the clouds to capture their own particular experience with physical detail or just come down the mountain a little lower and find some clearer pattern in the waves. For example: "The day we got the VCR our lives changed." or, "The United States is a great country, but it has one of the highest infant mortality rates in the world. Why?" Seeing compelling patterns gives the writer a reason to dig for details, and those details often encourage more reflection.

This model is not meant to present a formula for writing. Rather, it is simply a vague map of an ongoing process. Like the concept of a snapshot or new lead, it can provide students with opportunities to revise their work. For example, one question a peer might ask during a conference is, "Is there anywhere in your story where you could climb the mountain and reflect on the larger patterns?" or "Where do I need to dive into the sea for more details?"

For the first section of this chapter, I have focused on writing snapshots full of physical detail, which make up the sea of our experience. In the next section I will illustrate ways of teaching students to climb the mountain, reflecting and interpreting the patterns under the water.

Climbing the Mountain: Thoughtshots

I write to find out what I'm thinking about.

Edward Albee

"I want you to write down exactly what you are thinking right now. It doesn't have to be appropriate. We are not going to share it. You can throw it out after you have written it. Just put all your thoughts on the paper."

I'm in an eighth-grade class and many of the boys are crumpling their papers before the assignment is done. Some snicker at the words that come out of their brains.

We talk about the power writers have to tell their own thoughts and the thoughts of characters. Just as writers make physical snapshots, they can also take a snapshot of the thoughts in their characters' heads, or in their own mind. I teach the concept of the thoughtshot in both fiction and nonfiction writing.

A thoughtshot in fiction is simply a look at what a character is thinking and feeling. For example: "Brad wondered if Sarah ever loved him. There was a knot in his stomach as he walked up to the door." Similarly, in a personal narrative a thoughtshot is the reflections, thoughts, feelings, opinions of the author. It is when the author climbs the mountain and looks for the patterns under the waves. For example, "I have been trying to understand my sister for years and only recently did I discover she'd been trying to understand me too."

Thoughtshots often draw frames around stories and essays; they place events in a context and give the reader and the writer a reason to be interested. "It was my first night on the job as a pizza delivery man and I had a feeling it might be my last." In research writing, thoughtshots are often found in the first sentences of paragraphs. They are the skeleton on which the facts and examples are hung and from which unanswered questions grow: "Acid rain has far-reaching implications on the lives of our grandchildren."

To understand the difference between snapshots and thoughtshots a little better let's take a look at a brief passage from Katherine Paterson's novel *The Great Gilly Hopkins.* In this brief description Gilly, a foster child, is unpacking a suitcase at her latest foster home, and she takes out a snapshot of her mother. I've put what I would consider thoughtshots in italics.

Unpacking even just the few things in her brown suitcase, always seemed a waste of time to Gilly. She never knew if she'd be in a place long enough to make it worth the bother. And yet it was something to fill the time. There were two little drawers at the top and four larger ones below. She put her underwear in one of the little ones, and her shirts and jeans in one of the big ones, and then picked up the photograph from the bottom of the suitcase. (1987, p. 9)

Notice how Paterson skillfully moves from Gilly's thoughts to snapshots of the moment. In the last section of this chapter I'll talk more about how writers blend and tint thoughtshots with snapshots and vice versa, but before I do let's practice creating and inserting thoughtshots into nonfiction and fiction writing.

Influential People

1. Ask students to return to one of their snapshots of a person they wrote about earlier. Have students ask themselves this question: How has this person influenced my life?
2. Students write for ten minutes answering this question and others that arise.
3. Have students question conference their thoughtshot with a partner and turn one or two questions into a new lead.
4. Ask students to insert or add what they've written to their original snapshot or follow their new lead.

Thoughtshots In Fiction

1. Have students write a story about a character with a problem. It helps if the character is different than themselves but maybe the same age. Students then follow some of the note-taking steps at the beginning of this chapter to learn more about the character and find a good lead (if they want to). This exercise can also be done with a previously written draft as long as there is a main character in the story.
2. Ask students to freewrite the beginning of a story, making sure to double space and write on one side of the page.

3. Students read over the story and find one place to insert a thoughtshot of the character. It can be a mini-thoughtshot or a large one. Put a caret mark at the place and write the thoughtshot on the back of the page or on another piece of paper.

4. Students share the thoughtshots reflecting on how a character's thoughts bring the reader closer to the writing. New questions are discussed.

Thoughtshots in a Personal Narrative

1. Have students think of a childhood experience they remember well. They can make a web chart or just a list to help them think. Now ask them to freewrite a snapshot of that moment in the present tense as if they are still a child. (For example, "I stand on the warm diving board and stare down at the blue water.")

2. Ask students to read over what they wrote and write again for five minutes, telling the reader what this experience means to them now, as an older person.

3. Compare the two pieces. With any luck you can point out that the first deals more with immediate physical reality like a snapshot and the second deals with thoughts on looking back. Don't be surprised if this turns out to be the reverse, and don't chide a student for not doing the exercise in the way you described it. Simply point out the qualities in the writing that make up snapshots and thoughtshots. It's more important that they learn the general concept than to suppose there is a correct way to write a snapshot or thoughtshot.

4. Students insert a thoughtshot into a personal narrative they've already written. Have them pick a place where it makes sense to ask, "What was I thinking then?" or "What do I think now?"

Movies and television have dominated the imaginations of children for several generations now, yet people still read and book publishers continue to stay in business. Why? The answer is simple:

Writers can go deeper into minds than cameras. Think about it a moment. You are an author trying to convey a character's thoughts. With a camera you are limited to showing the character's face or actions. Maybe the character is thinking about the day he or she broke grandmother's fancy teapot with a slingshot and got locked in the closet. The movie director would have to flashback to the scene to show the character's thoughts. This is a disruptive technique and usually not worth doing unless the scene is very important.

In the sixties French New Wave film directors like François Truffaut and Jean Luc Goddard realized the limitations of movies when compared to literature, and they experimented with narrative voices that whispered thoughts between scenes. Their attempts to convey a novelistic quality to movies were partly successful, but the depth and complexity that comes naturally in literature must be spliced into a film. For this reason films always fall short of what literature can do. How many movies are better than the book? Books will never die because they can take us deeper and further into minds than any other artistic medium.

Understanding the nature of thoughtshots in literature is a wonderful way to teach students the alternative that books can provide them to the TV culture. It was Kurt Vonnegut, Jr., who said recently at a lecture at Syracuse University, "When we read we meditate with other minds." Students who love to write know this, and they can learn to appreciate the power of literature.

It was about twelve minutes before recess and I asked Taura if she could share her freewrite about her thoughts. She showed it to me. It was a short list of thoughts. The first was about recess and eating lunch, the second was about the dance on Saturday, the third was about who she would marry and how many children she should have, the fourth about her hatred of school. "Were you really thinking all that?" I asked, a little stunned by the range and complexity of her thoughts.

"That's only half of it," she said.

Spinoffs

- Ask students to write a short snapshot of a first time they did something, and then a thoughtshot of the same time and insert it.

- Students pick up an old story they have written, inserting one or two thoughtshots for their main character. (Remember, a thoughtshot doesn't have to be more than a sentence or two.)

- Students practice writing their thoughts in five-minute freewrites.

- Have students write about a general feeling like happiness or sadness, and then write two or three snapshots of times in their lives when they felt this.

Blending Thoughtshots with Snapshots

Your self is the totality of what you have lived. We can't just live in the present or we would be mindless. We live with the past.

Ruth Stone

For the sake of teaching I have presented thoughtshots and snapshots as separate entities. In reality, they are only techniques for breaking down and teaching narrative. Writers are constantly blending thoughts with physical realities and vice versa. However, defining each allows a writer to switch gears consciously.

For example, if the writer is only writing thoughtshots, chances are he could use a snapshot or two to ground the reader in a real setting. On the other hand, if writers are just writing snapshots, perhaps their writing could benefit from the introspection and personality development a thoughtshot brings to a character, or the larger purpose reflection can add to an essay. Or perhaps the writer could tint her snapshot with the emotions or thoughts of her character or herself. Writers learn to tint their snapshots with a character's feelings and vice versa. Novelist Thomas Williams once told me that writing was "what happens between the seer and the thing seen." I think we can see that Katherine Paterson knows this as she describes Gilly Hopkins looking at her long lost mother's photograph:

Out of the pasteboard frame and through the plastic cover the brown eyes of the woman laughed up at her as they always did. The glossy black hair hung in gentle waves without a hair astray. She looked as though she was the star of some TV show, but she wasn't. See—right there in the corner she had written, "For my beautiful Galadriel, I will always love you." She wrote that to me,

Gilly told herself, as she did each time she looked at it, only to me. She turned the frame over. (1987, p. 9)

In this passage Paterson skillfully shows us the world through Gilly's thoughts. Each sentence, except for the very last one I quoted, is a blend of snapshots colored with Gilly's feelings or thoughts about her mother. Learning to portray the objective world through the filter of their own emotions without revealing those emotions is a sophisticated and important skill. Try these advanced exercises with your class after they've explored thoughtshots and snapshots.

Tinting a Snapshot

1. Have students list twenty details of a place they know well. Some students might want to skip this part. Let them.

2. Students describe this place through the filter of one of the following emotions: 1) You just won ten million dollars in the Megabucks drawing. 2) You just accidentally murdered your best friend.

Important Rule: You must not mention anything about how you're feeling or talk about your thoughts or feelings in any way. Just describe the place.

3. Students share the descriptions. Point out how a strong description always ends up describing the author or character. Just as thoughtshots reflect the physical circumstances of a character's life, so snapshots through a character's eyes contain their thoughts and feelings.

Just as writers tint snapshots with emotions and thoughts, they also do the opposite. Imagine this: You are on a plane high above the Alaskan wilderness and the pilot has just had a heart attack and is now dead beside you. That's the situation in Gary Paulsen's novel *Hatchet.* Here's how Paulsen describes the internal world of his character without referring back to his situation:

The jolts that took the pilot had come, and now Brian sat and there was a strange feeling of silence in the thrumming roar of the engine—a strange feeling of silence and being alone. Brian was stopped.

He was stopped. Inside he was stopped. He could not think past what he saw, what he felt. All was stopped. The very core of him, the very center of Brian Robeson was stopped and stricken with a white-flash of horror, a terror so intense that his breathing, his thinking, and nearly his heart had stopped.

Stopped.

Seconds passed, seconds that became all of his life, and he began to know what he was seeing, began to understand what he saw and that was worse, so much worse that he wanted to make his mind freeze again.

He was sitting in a bushplane roaring seven thousand feet above the northern wilderness with a pilot who had suffered a massive heart attack and who was either dead or in something close to a coma.

He was alone.

In a roaring plane with no pilot he was alone.

Alone. (1987, p. 12)

Tinting a Thoughtshot

1. Tell students that something has happened to their character, something tragic or important in some way. Have them make a quick note of what that is, and then write a thoughtshot of that character's mind, without mentioning the thing that has happened.

2. Students share the thoughtshots, listening for their favorite details. Point out how the events of the day color the person's thoughts. Mention how a person's thoughts and feelings don't have to be about what is happening. Writers find metaphorical ways to portray inner feelings. For example, "There was an earthquake rumbling inside him."

Next time you read a novel or an essay, notice how the author weaves from his own mind or the mind of a character out into the physical universe and then back again. Point it out to students and invite them to explore and experiment with thoughtshots and snapshots. Teach them how to plunge into the sea of experience and write snapshots of rich, vivid detail, then to climb the mountain, writing ideas, reflections, feelings, and other thoughtshots. When writers are bored with a story, they are more often than not bored with how they are telling it. It's one thing to coerce a student to write with more detail and quite another to invite him or her to climb up into minds and then out into the world again.

Spinoffs

- Students think of a problem for a character, then pretend that character is asleep. They then write a dream that reflects that problem.
- Have students make a list of emotions. They then pick one and write a snapshot of the place they are sitting, tinting it with the emotion they chose.
- Give students a photocopied portion of a part of a novel, short story, or essay. Ask them to circle definite snapshots and/or thoughtshots. They needn't worry about identifying all the writing on the page. They can find a few passages that interest them. Talk about what everyone has found.
- Divide the class in two. Half writes simple snapshots of school hot lunch or any topic they choose. The other half writes thoughtshots. Share.
- Ask students to find an important moment in a story or essay they are ready to revise. Have them tint either a snapshot or a thoughtshot of that moment or just insert snapshots and thoughtshots. Instruct them to dig for details by asking themselves questions if they get stuck.

Don't Make a Scene! Build One

Dialogue, as much as anything else, reveals the character to the writer and, ultimately to the reader. I don't have a very clear idea of who the characters are until they start talking.

Joan Didion

A scene is dialogue mixed with description. In movie terms dialogue is the sound and description is the camera (a special camera that has an ESP X-ray zoom lens that can reveal a character's thoughts). Two people talking is pure dialogue, but when the author inserts thoughtshots and snapshots then we have the makings of a scene. Here's a scene from an essay my student Jan Wilson wrote for a college freshman English class. It's about a fight she had with her sister. If you like, read it to your class, pausing every so often to ask them if the last sentence you read was a snapshot, thoughtshot, or dialogue.

"Bet he kisses mushy and wet!" my sister taunted me. I twisted around and looked at her, my elbows deep in dishwater.

"Look—just finish your dinner and be quiet. He does not either." I didn't want to discuss my boyfriend, David, with my blabbermouth little sister. What did she know about kissing anyway?

Carol sat at the kitchen table, idly pushing the cold food around her plate. "Wet mushy kisses—wet mushy kisses—Janie loves David's wet mushy kisses," she singsonged to herself, but clearly intended for my ears.

"Stop it. You are one little smart aleck! Mom and Dad will get mad if they hear you," I warned, trying to distract her. Actually, I admitted to myself, David's kissing wasn't any bargain but I couldn't stand her needling me.

"Does he know you stuff your bra with Kleenex?" she teased, with that smug, know-it-all, expression on her face.

This was too much. My adolescent sensitivity burst with indignation. "I do not, you little dummy! Take this!" I scraped the soapsuds off my arms and picked up a quart of milk, shoving it in her face. "If you don't hush up and be quiet I'm going to pour this right over your head! Every last drop." The quart was nearly full.

"You wouldn't dare," she glowered. "Dad would kill you."

"You don't think so? I would, too. You're just asking for it."

"You're chicken! You'd never do it," she said assuredly, her eyes sparkling with excitement.

Very few professional authors even attempt to write more than a few lines of dialogue before inserting a snapshot or thoughtshot. One way to show the importance of inserting snapshots is to read Jan's scene without the thoughtshots or snapshots. Point out to students how thoughtshots and snapshots draw a frame around the dialogue.

Dialogue is just one aspect of a scene, and it's a general rule to use it, not to give information, but to reveal character. For example, it's far easier to say, "They said hello," than to write a page of dialogue where two characters say hello, but if that dialogue tells the reader something about the characters, then it's important to the story. When people speak they reveal themselves. What they fail to say is often as important as what they do say. Listen to this scene from playwright Roland Goodbody's one-act autobiographical play, *El Dia De Los Muertos*. Goodbody describes the transatlantic phonecall when he found out about his older brother's suicide.

I got the telephone call telling me of his death on a Wednesday evening in July, just after I got back from the A & P. It was my Dad. He seemed to be in a good mood, and I remember we talked about the weather for a bit. Then he asked if I was sitting down, and I said, "Yeah. As a matter of fact, I'm sitting on the floor. Why?"

"That's good, 'cos I've got some bad news for you."

"Oh yeah, what's that, then?" I said. I thought he was joking because of the way he said it. But he didn't answer me; he just made a sort of strangled sound in his throat. And then there was silence.

Ralph came on the line. "Hello, Roland."

"Ralph, what's going on? Is the old man okay? One minute he's talking to me and the next he just walks off and leaves the phone. Is he drunk?"

"No, he's not drunk."

"Well, what's happening then? He said he had some bad news to tell me. Do you know what it was?"

"Look, I'll put Mark on, all right?"

And then Mark says, "Hello, where've you been? We've been trying to call you for hours. You been out on the town again?"

"No, I haven't been out on the town again! It's about six o'clock here, isn't it? I've just done a bit of shopping. Look, what the hell is going on there? First Dad's on the phone, then Ralph, and now you. What's this about some bad news he was trying to tell me? Do you know?"

"Yeah," he said. "Trevor's dead," and he choked a bit.

I kept the receipt from the A & P.

With a few simple brush strokes of dialogue Goodbody illustrates a family's inability to accept the loss of a son. For a moment, imagine how much weaker this scene would be if Goodbody replaced the dialogue with a snapshot or thoughtshot. "My family called me on the phone but none of them would tell me what was wrong . . ." A line or two of dialogue in the right place can do more that a thousand pages of description.

Natalie Babbitt uses mostly dialogue and snapshots to introduce her main character Winnie to Jesse Tuck in the novel *Tuck Everlasting*. Notice how Babbitt skillfully slips in several mini-thoughtshots so that we can feel Winnie's attraction to Tuck:

For a long moment they looked at each other in silence, the boy with his arm still raised to his mouth. Neither of them moved. At last his arm fell to his side. "You may as well come out," he said, with a frown.

Winnie stood up, embarrassed and, because of that, resentful. "I didn't mean to watch you," she protested as she stepped into the clearing. "I didn't know anyone would be here."

The boy eyed her as she came forward. "What're *you* doing here?" he asked her sternly.

"It's my wood," said Winnie, surprised by the question. "I can come here whenever I want to. At least, I was never here before, but I *could* have come, any time."

"Oh," said the boy, relaxing a little. "You're one of the Fosters, then."

"I'm Winnie," she said. "Who are you?"

"I'm Jesse Tuck," he answered. "How do." And he put out a hand.

Winnie took his hand, staring at him. He was even more beautiful up close. "Do you live nearby?" she managed at last, letting go of his hand reluctantly. "I never saw you before. Do you come here a lot? No one's supposed to. It's our wood." Then she added quickly, "It's all right, though, if *you* come here. I mean, it's all right with *me*." (1975, pp. 26–27)

Once I've introduced the students to all the elements that make up scenes, I show them how to build and rebuild them in their stories. I sometimes start by handing each student a lump of play-dough and telling them to make something. Then I ask them how many people made something right away and were content and how many people changed it around. Most enjoy playing with playdough and changing their creations. I say the same is true of writers building scenes. Many writers talk of the joy of molding and shaping scenes, and following are a couple of ways to get students tinkering.

Living Narrative

1. Working with your class, think up a scene where one character has a secret from another. It could be a child afraid to tell a parent about a bad report card or a car crash, or a parent who has to tell a child about a divorce, or a shy guy or girl trying to ask a girl or guy out on a date. I usually begin by picking a volunteer and saying to the class, "This is _____ and she has a secret. What's her [fictional] name? What's the secret? This is our main character and because it's her point of view she is the only character whose thoughts will be revealed. (Note: you could reveal the thoughts of both characters if you are not interested in teaching point of view.) Once we've got the secret and the two characters I ask for a few volunteers to fill in other roles.

2. Assign roles as follows:

Character a: voice

Character b: voice

Character a's thoughts: what he/she is thinking

Character b's thoughts: what he/she is thinking

Snapshot painter: Physically describes the scene, the characters, and their actions. One tip for the snapshot painter is to focus on what the character does with his or her hands.

Director: You should assign yourself this role until students see how it works. The director simply points to the part of the narrative he or she wishes to speak. In essence the director is the writer calling on the aspects of craft.

3. At this point I tell the class, "You are all braincells in the head of a writer. I am the director and will point to a character or that character's thoughts or to my snapshot painter. That person is going to say his or her part or call on one of you for help or both. (Note: It's very important that you insist that no one blurts out, as this exercise can be a recipe for chaos without this rule.)

4. Arrange the scene in front of the class with thoughtshot narrators several paces behind their characters. The snapshot narrator should be off to the side. As director you have a choice. You can stand on a chair or simply off to one side. You need to be in sight line of both the actors and the audience.

5. As you act out the scene remember that the secret should not be revealed until the very end. This will give the scene more tension. Have fun!

(Optional: You may want to ask a student or aide to write down the scene so you can read it back later. You may also want to add more characters to your scene as you go along.)

Sample Scene

(I've written this out in dramatic form to model the exercise, but it could also be written simply as prose.)

Sarah was not supposed to go out with Spike and now she's coming home late from the dance and her parents suspect she may have been driven by Spike on his Harley.

Sarah's thoughts: They'll never know if I don't tell them. Why do I always feel like I have to be honest with them. Susan Brown isn't with her parents and they never find out. Not like those TV shows where the parents always find out in the end.

Snapshot: Sarah stood by the front door, her hair blowing in all directions. She could still hear the faint sound of Spike's Harley hitting third gear as he hit Main Street. She opened the door and sneaked into the hallway. Her feet sank into the carpet.

Sarah's thoughts: It's late, dammit. I knew we should have left earlier. If I could just get to my room I could tell them I was in bed already.

Mom: Sarah, is that you?

Sarah: Uh huh.

Snapshot: Mom stood in her pink bathrobe by the doorway to the flourescent kitchen. Her face was white and her eyes red.

Sarah: Gee, I'm sorry it's so late. Cheryl's car wouldn't start and we had to call her father.

Snapshot: Sarah held her hands behind her back and shifted side to side on her feet.

Mom: What happened to your hair? Was there a hurricane?

Sarah: Oh, Mom, you know how kids are. They kept all the windows open.

Snapshot: Sarah pulled her hair together in a ponytail and let it fall over her back.

Mom: Tell me about it. You were with Spike, weren't you?

Thoughtshot: Sarah felt as if the floor was moving like a ship caught in an ocean swell. I will tell her, she thought. I always tell her.

Sarah: What a ridiculous thing to say!

Snapshot: Mom walked to the cupboard and took out a bottle of aspirin.

6. Teach students how to act out scenes in their own stories, paying particular attention to all the elements at work.

Build a Scene

1. Find a book with a scene in it that demonstrates the elements above. Read students the dialogue without the narration and the narration without the dialogue. Talk about how authors build scenes with dialogue, snapshots, and thoughtshots.

2. Ask students to create a situation where one character has a secret from another character or a situation where there is tension between two characters. Don't let the secret get revealed in the dialogue. Let the characters' words tell more about what they don't say. Write the dialogue skipping two lines to leave plenty of room to go back and add thoughtshots and snapshots. (This exercise works well with pairs. Students can play the roles of each character. If you choose to do it with pairs, ask both partners to write down the complete dialogue. This way they can revise it differently if they choose to work alone for later sections of this exercise.)

3. Have students insert at least two snapshots and thoughtshots wherever they think it may be important to reveal something about their main character. Ask students to make their snapshots and thoughtshots more than just participial phrases like, " 'Get up!' Matt said, standing by the door." Writing snapshots and thoughtshots with full sentences in the past tense usually makes for stronger writing. Here is my revision: " 'Get up,' Matt said. He stood by the door with his hand on the gold knob. His face was bright red." Model this a few times for students.

4. Have students act out the scenes in front of the class or simply read them.

5. After the students have done one reading, have them read their pieces again, pausing between lines of dialogue to add snapshots and thoughtshots. (When a scene is acted, classes usually have fun inserting snapshots because all they have to do is describe the actions of the actors.)

6. Ask how many students enjoyed adding snapshots and thoughtshots to their scenes. Tell them how happy you are that they are learning what many professional writers know: revision can be fun!

"But what if they write too much dialogue?" the seventh-grade teacher asks me. "Their stories go on and on, the two characters talking back and forth like some prolonged tennis match. What do I do?"

I stand in front of the class and give my speech on dialogue, using the overhead projector. Most writers are not talented enough to write really convincing dialogue. It's difficult to write the way people speak and not always necessary to include it in a story. However, we've learned today that a scene can still work if the writer balances dialogue with thoughtshots of one or more characters and/or snapshots.

It's also very easy to cut dialogue and replace it with either thoughtshots or snapshots. For example, let's say two characters are saying goodbye.

"Well, I guess I'll see you later."

"OK, Bill."

"Bye, now."

"See you later."

This unrevealing interchange can easily be replaced with, "Bill and Fred said goodbye."

Dialogue is easy and fun to cut out of stories, and if it doesn't leave a hole, it's a good idea to do so. Most writers learn to use dialogue in small doses, using it more as a way of developing character than a means of progressing the story. If the old codger you are writing about goes to Dunkin Donuts and says to the waitress, "Pour me a cup of that Mississippi mud, would you honey," that tells me something about him as opposed to the narrator saying, "He ordered a cup of coffee." However, if that same character is saying goodbye to his friend, and the exchange is rather unrevealing like the dialogue above, it may be better to advance the story with a line or two of description like, "They said goodbye."

In an essay the same guidelines apply. Essayists choose very carefully the places where they add scenes; they need only be inserted at moments very central to the point writers try to make.

Here are a few questions to help authors decide to build a scene or cut a scene.

1. Does the dialogue tell us something about the characters?

2. Do we learn something new about the main character by what he or she thinks in reaction to something another character says?

3. Is the action of the story pushed along by the scene or does the scene slow it down? (Note: All scenes slow down stories, but powerful scenes have a reason. They reveal characters or relationships or something important about the plot.)

4. If you cut the scene out of the story does it leave a hole?

Here's a way to teach kids how to cut dialogue.

Cutting Dialogue

1. Have students find or write a piece of prolonged dialogue, making it really boring and banal. Then model the cutting process on an overhead projector. Remind your students that they can replace pages of dialogue with one sentence. Model this for your class as follows:

"Hi, Joe."
"Hi, Sarah."
"Where are you going?"
"School. Where are you going?"
"School."
"Can I walk with you?"
"Sure."

Replace with: Joe and Sarah said hello and chit-chatted for a while, and then Sarah asked if she could walk with him.

2. Have students write a dialogue of two people talking about something boring like the weather. Just write the dialogue and double-space between lines. (They can also use a scene from a story they've already written if it has a lot of dialogue.)

3. Ask students to circle the lines of dialogue they like best and replace other lines of dialogue with snapshots or thought-shots. Have them build a scene out of the lines that they keep by adding snapshots and thoughtshots.

Example: Joe and Sarah talked a lot about school, Mrs. Horrigan, and how they hated all the homework she gave on the weekends. They complained about little brothers and little sisters for a while, but as they got closer to school Joe knew it was now or never. "Sarah," he said, as they walked past the brick wall that the school sign hung on.
    "What?" Sarah replied. "Rat got your tongue?"
    He wanted to laugh because it was funny. She was always coming up with things like that. But he couldn't laugh because the words were trying to make their way out of his mouth.
    "The school dance," he said. His voice was like a squeaky door trying to open.
    "What about the school dance?"
    "Will you go with me?"

4. Have students share finished scenes and the process of adding and subtracting. Point out to students the joy of cutting boring dialogue and encourage them to put this on their editing checklists.

Building scenes is one of the best ways to get young writers revising. Whether it's a question of inserting a snapshot of the coffee cup that holds the poison or inserting dialogue of your little sister yelling for Dad, scenes gives students a feel for the nuances of craft that make a story come alive. In the next chapter, I will show you how to teach students to integrate what we've learned so far to manipulate time in their writing.

Spinoffs

• Have students write a dialogue between siblings who are fighting with each other. Have them go back and insert mini-snapshots and thoughtshots.

• Photocopy a scene from a book the class has read. Ask students to pretend they are the author and have decided to get rid of all the dialogue. Students write a paragraph that tells the scene instead of showing it.

• Students write a scene about something that happened that day between them and a friend. Ask them to make the snapshots in between the dialogue as vivid as they can.

• Have students write a dramatic scene where two characters confront each other. Make the tension last by adding plenty of snapshots and thoughtshots.

• Ask students to go back through their writing and find a story with too much dialogue. Have them cut as much as they can and insert thoughtshots and snapshots to tighten up the scene.

• Students write a play made up of several scenes. When they're done with it, ask them to revise it into a story by simply adding thoughtshots and snapshots.

Explode a Moment and Shrink a Century

Playing with Time

Time to a writer is like playdough
in the hands of a toddler.
Barry Lane

The bases were loaded and it was up to him, but the coach asked him not to swing at the ball. He wondered why until he heard the coach whisper to the assistant coach, "They'll never strike out that shrimp." Jon was short and up to that moment he was very proud to be on the Little League team, but when he realized he was only on the first string because he was short and too difficult to strike out, he was very hurt.

Jon was a student in my freshman English class. In his first draft of an essay about this experience he wrote, "It really broke my heart when the coach said that and because of that I walked up to the plate and struck out on purpose."

In conference I asked Jon to locate the big moment in the story. It was when the coach whispered to the other coach, "They'll never strike out that shrimp." I asked Jon to make that moment last as long as he could, because the more he could describe that moment, the more the reader would become him and feel the impact of the story. This is a paraphrase of what he wrote.

I could feel my cheeks flush red with embarrassment. I reached down and picked up the bat. It was cold in my hands. I looked up at the stands and I could see my father cheering. He was thrusting his fist up in the air and shouting something I couldn't understand. I looked at the pitcher. The ball was moving up and out of his glove following his hand in one fluid motion. I swung before it was halfway there. 'Stee-rike,' the empire shouted. . . .

I tell students that when Jon says, "What the coach said broke my heart," the reader says, "Poor Jon." But the more Jon describes the big moment in his story in great detail, the more the reader becomes Jon, and his essay begins to do justice to the emotions that underpin it.

Several years ago I had lunch with the novelist Ernest Hebert. He had recently begun teaching his first creative writing class and was struggling to find concepts from his work as a writer to help him teach. He told me that the number-one best concept for helping students to revise their short stories was what he called "the significant moment." "What is the significant moment in the story?" he would ask his students. If there was one it often needed more attention (as with Jon's story), and if there wasn't one it frequently meant there wasn't a real story yet and the author had to think more about who the main character was and what conflicts and changes were going on.

Hebert's idea was not new to me. I had originally learned the writer's power to manipulate time from Sue Wheeler, a fiction writer at the University of New Hampshire. More recently I met Ilene Wax, a reading teacher from Halifax, Vermont, who calls this same exercise "exploding a moment" because the writer takes a sentence or two and explodes it, scattering details all over the page. Now that we know about snapshots, thoughtshots, and scenes, we have some powerful tools for exploding moments.

Here's how Jan Wilson exploded the moment when she poured a quart of milk over her sister's head in the essay titled "Sisters," from which I quoted in the last chapter:

I watched myself begin this horrible deed. My hand seemed to suddenly have a will of its own. It picked up the milk carton. The spout was already open. My arm extended over Carol's head, tipping the carton. The liquid poured in slow, steady thick unending stream down through her long blonde hair, soaking the back of her clothes and running onto the floor. As the milk reached the floor I shifted the spout slightly to begin another long milky journey down the front of her. It poured over her forehead, in the eyes, running in rivers down each side of her nose, converging on the chin and splashing into her plate. Her food was soon awash and the milk poured over the edge, and ran into her lap. And still I poured on— it was too late to stop now. The rapture of it all. Oh, sweet revenge.

Carol was shocked into absolute silence, her milk-washed eyes staring at me in total disbelief—almost uncomprehending. What had I done? I only meant to pour a little to scare her and now it was all over—everywhere. Her chair was a four-legged island in the middle of a giant white pond in the kitchen floor. How could one quart of milk go so far? For a second or two she didn't react and I had a brief but fleeting prayer that she was stunned speechless. However, not for long.

"Daddeeeeeeeeeeeeeeeeee!" she screamed at the top of her lungs. The sound of cocktail glasses being knocked over the coffee table in the living room and my father charging around the corner happened almost simultaneously. In an instant he took in the whole scene. Horrible big sister pours milk over innocent little sister's head. I simply couldn't have looked much worse. It didn't take any smarts to realize that. I knew there was no way of explaining my way out of this one. "Guilty" was the immediate verdict of the judge. My mother, the long since powerless "jury" of one, as usual, did not interfere.

My father, in self-righteous splendor, straightened to his full 6'6" of height, and livid with rage, dragged me into my bedroom, stripping off his belt on the way. I tried to escape his iron grip, to no avail. I had the horrible impression this was going to be a beating I'd never forget.

Notice how Jan makes the moment when she poured the milk last with a very long snapshot of the milk's journey down her sister's face. When I read this piece to students we usually discuss how long it takes to pour a quart of milk over your sister's head. I usually ask, "Why doesn't she just say, 'Then I dumped the milk over my sister's head and she was a real mess'?" "She wants to make the moment last," they usually reply. I then tell students how Jan really dug for physical details to prolong that moment. She asked herself questions like we did in chapters 2 and 3 of this book. Exploding moments pulls detail out of writers naturally. It gets writers digging deeper for thoughtshots, snapshots, dialogue—anything to slow that moment down. At the end of her essay, Jan Wilson exploded another moment that brought home some of the terror and sadness children feel growing up in an alcoholic household. Notice how Jan pulls the reader into her childhood with snapshots, thoughtshots, and dialogue:

Later, laying on the bed, my whole body agonized with pain. The least movement brought more tears to my eyes and I could feel the welts raising on my back. I couldn't imagine being able to get up, much less walk to school the next day.

The door creaked open and by the light from the hall Carol crept across the room. "Oh, Janie, Janie," she whispered, bending over me. "I'm sorry, I didn't mean to do it." She didn't mean to do what? I asked her. Yell for Daddy, she said. Her tears splashed on my face as she put her arms around my shoulders, hugging me gently. I struggled up on one elbow and wrapped an arm around her. "It's O.K., Carol. Don't worry," I crooned, trying to comfort her. She seemed so small, frightened and confused.

We wept together, quietly, in the darkened bedroom—clinging to each other in near desperation. The only other sound was the faint tinkle of ice cubes in the kitchen as the next round of drinks was being mixed.

Acting Out an Exploded Moment

If you enjoyed acting out a scene with your class, try acting out an exploded moment. Begin by reading an exploded moment from literature students have been reading. Here's one from Elizabeth George Speare's young adult novel, *The Sign of the Beaver:*

> There was a crashing of bush and a low, snarling growl. An immense paw reached through the thicket and tumbled the cub over and out of sight. In its place loomed a huge brown shape. Bursting through the leaves was a head three times as big as the cubs. No curiosity in those small eyes, only an angry reddish gleam.
>
> Somehow Matt had the sense not to run. He stood frozen on the path. A bear could overtake a running man in a few bounds. And this one was only two bounds away. The bear's head moved slowly from side to side. Its heavy body brushed aside the branches as though they were cobwebs. It swayed, shifting its weight from one foot to the other. Slowly it rose on its hind legs. Matt could see the wicked curving claws.
>
> Matt would never know why he acted as he did. He could not remember thinking at all, only staring with numb horror at the creature about to charge. Somehow he did move. He swung the dead rabbit by its ears and hurled it at the bear's head. The tiny body struck the bear squarely on the nose. With a jerk of the head the bear shook it off as though it were a buzzing mosquito. The rabbit flopped useless to the ground. The bear did not even bother to look down at it. (1983, pp. 72–73)

1. Point out to students how Speare (or an author of your choice) uses mostly snapshots and a few thoughtshots. Go to the board or overhead and ask the class to pretend to be the author by continuing to explode the moment. Push students to dig for details; help them along if you need to. Turn their details into sentences and those sentences into paragraphs. When you have a paragraph or two written down, read it out loud, and then turn back to the book and compare what you've done with what the author has.

2. Pick which scene you prefer and act it out, using the roles

of main character, thoughts, and snapshot painter as mentioned in the last chapter. With yourself as director, ask students to dig hard for details to make the moment last as long as possible.

3. After you've modeled being the director, try it again with a student directing.

4. Act out and explode moments from your students' stories. Let the student writer be the director.

Time Is a Stretch of Mountains

I always begin teaching students about time and writing by asking this one question: "What would it be like if you could live the same way you write?" We explore all the great things one could do, like reaching into your pocket and pulling out the winning Megabucks ticket, or a million-dollar bill, or anything students fancy. Then I tell students of a quote I have heard from more than one famous writer: "Fiction writers are the children who get sent to their rooms for telling stories. Eventually they find a pen and a piece of paper up in their room and start writing the stories down."

We can't live the way we write and expect to stay out of trouble, but do we have to write the same way we live? If you want to write about something that happened in the afternoon do you have to start in the morning? No, you don't. As a writer you choose what you want to put in and what you want to leave out.

When we write, our entire lives are like a stretch of mountains and we can choose where to dwell. So, if I'm going to write about something that happened on an afternoon in June, I don't have to start my story with the alarm clock buzzing in the morning of that day. I can jump right to the afternoon like this: "It was the worst afternoon of my life." Once there I can dwell for pages on one moment that only lasted five seconds. Likewise, I can use one sentence to skip over large areas of time in order to get closer to my story: "He saw Janet several times over the next three months, but nothing would prepare him for what would happen the night of the dance. It was a snowy night and his father had trouble starting the car. . . . "

Once students understand the basic power they have in writing that they don't have in living, they're ready to apply some of the concepts we've learned in this book to both explode moments and shrink time. This next exercise is a more logical way to teach students to explode a moment. To this day, it's one of the best exercises I've found for drawing pertinent detail out of students.

Exploding a Moment

1. Explain to students that writing is different from living. In real life, we can't rearrange reality and expect to get away with it, but as writers we have more freedom. When we write we need not do it the same way that we live, one moment at a time. As we learned in chapter 1 when we talked about leads, we can jump right to the time that interests us the most. We also learned this when we cut dialogue in chapter 4. Explain that writers can spend one sentence to cover years, such as: "After ten years he came back from England," and pages covering one important moment (Jon's moment on the baseball team or Jan's moment dumping the milk). Find some of your own examples of exploded moments from books in your classroom.

2. Tell the students that they are going to practice writing in slow motion. Ask if they can think of a moment in a film where slow motion is used. You'll probably hear answers like, "Someone is shooting someone else," "Something is exploding," or "The big race."

An example of a slightly longer moment of time I mention is the opening sequence of the movie *ET*. Most students have seen it, and I ask them to recall all the details the film-maker uses. We make a list.

the jangly keys
the searchlights
the corn field
the lights of the city beneath

I explain that all film directors do what's known as a storyboard. They have an artist draw pictures of each camera angle before they even start the movie. Each picture is like a detail for a writer, only writers have a special camera that can record smells, thoughts, feelings, and more.

3. Ask students to think of a dramatic moment in time that lasted only a few seconds or minutes but was very important to them. It can be something sad or scary, like a car accident, or happy, like coming down the stairs on Christmas morning, or confusing, like the very first time they held their baby brother in their arms. Have them brainstorm a short list or discuss moments with their partner or write the word ME in the middle of a blank page and web five explodable moments from their life.

(Note: This assignment often stirs deep emotions, so be prepared to help reassure students that it's okay to write about personal pain.)

4. Students fill a whole page freewriting for fifteen minutes about that one moment that lasted only a few seconds to a minute. Remind them that every detail they can think of will make that moment come alive and last longer. If they get stuck, have them ask a question like, "What was I thinking?" or "What color was the ceiling?" They can blend snapshots with thoughtshots and/or a scene. Urge them to go back in time and re-enter their younger self.

Important: Remind students they are only writing about one short moment. They are not allowed to go to the next day, unless, of course, their writing takes off.

5. Ask students to stop and read over their freewrite and circle their favorite detail. Have them add three more details at the bottom of the page.

6. Break the class into small groups. Have them share pieces with the group and have a question conference on paper. Students should keep all questions in their folder with their piece.

7. Using the questions, students add detail to their moment or turn the best question into a new lead and follow it for another ten minutes, exploding the same moment.

8. (Optional) Try acting out a student's exploded moment. Revise through acting.

Several weeks ago I asked some teachers how their students revised. One woman said, "I ask them questions like, 'Don't you think you could expand a little bit here?'" When we examine this question closer we see that it's not a question at all, but more of a command. The student might do what the teacher says, and in doing so even make a story stronger, but whose story would it be? If this same teacher had successfully taught the concept of "Exploding a moment" she would only have to ask her student one question: "Is there a significant moment in your story?" If the student could locate it and knew the power of going in slow motion, using techniques like snapshots, thoughtshots, and dialogue, chances are he might volunteer to explode that moment all on his own. An even more effective approach might be to have students find each other's big moments in peer conferences. (See spin-offs.)

If we are to truly empower students as writers and critics we need to give them a fully comprehensible language of craft that will help them to assess and redefine their efforts. We need to model for them the power they have in writing that they don't have in life.

Here are three more examples of exploded moments in writing.

Fifth grader Jodi Martelle doesn't explode one short moment, but a series of moments. In revision she might decide to zero in on the big moment when the trucks drive away.

It was 4:00 am of a cold saturday morning in January. We were going to see my cousin take off to Massachusetts and then to Saudi Arabia. We were at the air base in Burlington, VT. When my mom got in the door she started to cry. I could feel the urge to cry but I held it in. All my relatives were there. Finally we went into the big cold room where we would see them go. Everyone was crying but I held it in. I felt like a walking teddy bear because I would walk over to someone and they would give me a hug, then to another person and the same thing would happen. It was now 6:30 and I was now the official helmet holder—not for very long because that thing weighed a ton. We had brought flags. One for my cousin Todd and one for us to wave at him. When it was finally time to go we all went outside and waved as they drove in their big, big truck. I felt my heart drop and get heavy when they went away and I remember this like it was yesterday.

Nan McBroom, a fourth-grade teacher from Roxbury Village School, exploded the brief moment before she answered the phone call that told of her father's death. Notice how Nan uses thoughtshots to draw the reader into her sense of panic.

There was darkness, it was pitch black, the moonless morning of April 12, 1972. I heard the telephone ringing; I was hoping and praying for the obscene phone call. As I pulled myself out of bed I noticed a reflection from the light of my Woolworth's alarm clock—3:15 am. Something's wrong, no one calls at this time; it must be a prank, no, this logic didn't help. The pit in my stomach got heavier and heavier. I picked my way past the bed, feeling for my robe. I was sure I left it over the chair. Please hang up. It can't be that important; what wouldn't wait until morning? Flashes—an accident, yes, my brother, seventeen; he's wild. Maybe he's hurt, dead. Oh, it must be a wrong number, nothing bad ever happens to my family. I slipped on my robe and groped my way toward the sounds of the ring. Why didn't I listen to the customer service representative from Ma Bell and put that extension next to the bed. More flashes entered my head—the pit grew wider as I thought of the security of parents, even at the age of 24 I still depended on them though I talked of independence and freedom from home. I feel the cold hardwood floor of the hallway. I'm almost to the ringing destination. Finally, I reach the study, feeling up and down the wall—the smooth plaster, a light switch.

Fifth grader Isaac Mayo exploded the moment before he jumped off the high dive for the first time. Notice how his careful observation adds to the suspense:

The first dive

My hand trembled as it touched the cold metal of the ladder. I looked up and it seemed the ladder would never end. I raised my left foot and as it touched the first rung, the step shifted and squeaked under my weight. I lifted my right foot and set it down next to the first. Together they slowly warmed the metal platform underneath them. I shivered at the thought of what I was about to do. I raised up my left foot and began the long slow climb, one cold, squeaky step after another. Finally at the top, I looked out at the vast expanse of water in front of me. Carefully, I inched my feet forward along the bumpy road of fiberglass. Reaching the end of the board, I thought about the fact that I was 15 feet above the surface of the water! I must be crazy! I decided I had to do it. Gently, I started to bounce a little, just letting the board vibrate under my feet. Soon, my feet began to leave the bumpy surface of fiberglass for a fraction of a second each time I sprang my knees. With each bounce the distance grew greater as the board pushed up under my feet. Suddenly, I was in flight and at the apex of my jump, I thrust my body out away from the board. My eyes were squeezed shut and I wondered when I would hit the water. The wind was hitting my face and then suddenly it was the clean, coolness of the water. It washed over my body as I glided through its depth and started gracefully back up towards the sparkling surface. With a shout of triumph, I broke out of the water ready to test myself again.

With older students I use what I still regard as the best exploded moment in literature, the moment in George Orwell's essay, "Shooting an Elephant." The moment when Orwell shoots an elephant simply because a thousand Burmese people are screaming for him to do so. Orwell spends several pages describing approximately five seconds of action. Literary critics often allude to Orwell's description of the dying elephant as symbolic of the crumbling, slightly senile, British Empire. Notice how Orwell cleverly tints his snapshot of the dying elephant with details that evoke, but don't tell, his feelings about the Empire:

When I pulled the trigger I did not hear the bang or feel the kick—one never does when the shot goes home—but I heard the devilish roar of glee that went up from the crowd. In that instant, in too short a time, one would have thought, even for the bullet to get there, a mysterious, terrible change had come over the elephant. He neither stirred nor fell, but every line of his body had altered. He looked suddenly stricken, shrunken, immensely old, as though the frightful impact of the bullet had paralysed him without knocking him down. At last, after what seemed a long time—it might have been five seconds, I dare say—he sagged flabbily to his knees. His mouth slobbered. An enormous senility seemed to have settled upon him. One could have imagined him thousands of years old. I fired again into the same spot. At the second shot he did not collapse but climbed with desperate slowness to his feet and stood weakly upright, with legs sagging and head drooping. I fired a third time. That was the shot that did for him. You could see the agony of it jolt his whole body and knock the last remnant of strength from his legs. But in falling he seemed a moment to rise, for as his hind legs collapsed beneath him he seemed to tower upward like a huge rock toppling, his trunk reaching skywards like a tree. (1950, p. 10)

Shrink a Century

After you've taught students to explode moments, try getting them to shrink time. This can be a more difficult concept to grasp so you may need to model it several times.

Read students a passage where the author compresses time into a paragraph or two. Try finding passages in books from your classroom. Here's an example of shrinking a large block of time from the sixth chapter of E. B. White's classic, *Charlotte's Web*.

Notice how E. B. White not only compresses time, he characterizes it by giving specific examples to help the reader feel how Fern felt.

> The early summer days on the farm are the happiest and fairest days of the year. Lilacs bloom and make the air sweet, and then fade. Apple blossoms come with the lilacs, and the bees visit around among the trees. The days grow warm and soft. School ends, and children have time to play and to fish for trout in the brook. Avery often brought a trout home in his pocket, warm and stiff and ready to be fried for supper.
>
> Now that school was over, Fern visited the barn, almost every day, to sit quietly on her stool. The animals treated her as an equal. The sheep lay calmly at her feel.
>
> Around the first of July, the work horses were hitched to the mowing machine, and Mr. Zuckerman climbed into the seat and drove into the field. All morning you could hear the rattle of the machine as it went round and round, while the tall grass fell down behind the cutter bar in long green swathes. Next day, if there was no thunder shower, all hands would help rake and pitch and load, and the hay would be hauled to the barn in the high hay wagon, with Fern and Avery riding on top of the load. (1952, 42)

White goes on for several pages giving more examples of early summer days, but to model compressing time, ask your students to brainstorm some of their own examples of those first warm days of summer. Write them on the board and with your students' help, turn them into a paragraph or two. After you've read your paragraph back to the class, turn to page 43 in *Charlotte's Web* and begin reading the second paragraph, which begins with the sentence, "Early summer days are a jubilee time for birds. . . ." Remark about the process of a writer digging for examples to characterize a large chunk of time.

Sometimes students blank out at finding a piece of time in their lives. I tell them, "Fine, do your whole life, but search for the moments that give it character." Here is an example from Joe, one of the men in my prison writing class.

> I was born in 1963 and lived in Vergennes, VT. I lived with my mother and father and one sister in a little apartment over a

creamy stand. I don't remember exactly how long we lived their though.

We moved into a house down the road a little ways. I remember going to school and how much I hated it. I don't remember most of my grade school years or my childhood either. I can remember a time that I broke some windows one day. I got into a lot of trouble for that. I don't know why I broke them.

Joe's memories start out being vague and boring but eventually they lead him to something interesting. Why did he break those windows that day? If students say they can't remember, tell them to write about that and with any luck it will lead them to a memory.

Think Shrink

Now that you've modeled several approaches with students let's begin compressing time.

1. Ask students to list interesting blocks of time in their life, like that summer at camp, the months after little sister was born, a school year to remember. Have them try characterizing each block of time with one adjective like *confusing, angry, happy, wild,* or anything that comes to mind.

2. Ask students to freewrite for ten minutes about that time. Have them try to include at least three examples of events that happened. Write snapshots as well as thoughtshots.

3. Have students share and question-conference.

4. Ask them to insert more detail of events and memories into their pieces, using their questions.

5. Students find a story in their folder that they feel is too long and boring. Have them circle the boring parts and shrink them to a sentence or two. For example, a page-long description of breakfast might evolve into, "After a long, uneventful breakfast the phone rang and I knew it was Sheila."

6. (Optional) Ask students to try exploding one moment from the time they wrote about.

As writers develop concepts of craft they learn to manipulate reality to achieve power and emphasis in their work. Instead of the mindless dictation that teachers sometimes refer to as "breakfast-to-bed" stories, students begin to see they can choose what they want to put in or explode and, perhaps even more important, what they want to leave out.

Spinoffs

- Ask students to find a partner and swap stories. They can find the big moment in each other's story and write three questions that will help the author find more details. Then they use the questions to explode the moment.
- Have students find an exploded moment from a published novel or story. Ask students to generate a list of questions that they might want to know more about. On a blank piece of paper students then revise the author's exploded moment.
- Have students find a draft of a story. Ask them to find an explodable moment or shrinkable chunk of time in the story. Students then explode a moment or shrink time on a separate piece of paper and make an insert mark where it goes in the story.
- Do a story circle where each child tells the same story but adds a new sentence or two. After the story has ended ask the group if there was a big moment. Agree on one and then go around again taking turns exploding that one moment.
- Ask students to explode a moment from history that they've experienced. Some moments might be: The space shuttle blowing up, President Reagan being shot, the Berlin Wall crumbling, the Persian Gulf War.
- For a social studies assignment, have students think of a decade like the sixties, seventies, or eighties. They can shrink that decade into a page or two of writing, and dig for specific details to make their time compression some alive. If the students enjoy doing this, ask them to shrink an entire century, again using specific examples to make their ideas come alive.
- Try the following:

  a. Ask students to explode a moment with just snapshots.

  b. Have students explode a moment with just thoughtshots.

  c. Have students shrink a chunk of time with just thoughtshots.

d. Have students shrink the same time with just snapshots.

e. Have students cut and paste combining the two.

- Tell students to shrink their favorite or worst season into a couple of paragraphs.
- Tell students to explode one moment that characterizes their favorite or worst season.

Friction or Nonfriction

Finding Form in Writing and Reading

Invention is a form of organization.
Graham Greene

Peter knows what a story is. It's when the new guy in town has to face up to the school bully. Sarah knows it's that morning when her father told her that her grandmother died and she had to think about what it would be like to never see her again. Kelly remembers the day she locked her little sister in a closet and she almost suffocated. Sure, all stories and essays are about change, conflict, and resolution. They have beginnings, middles, and ends, and there's usually some central question or moral that the author is trying to figure out or express. But a teacher can usually tell without reading a word when students have a story in their bones. It's a look they get in their eyes; it's how they sit scribbling when it's time for class to end. It's how they're mesmerized by the book in their lap even though the lunch bell has just rung.

In my travels, I hear teachers complain that their students rarely face the task of revising with the enthusiasm they show when writing a first draft. I tell them it's the same way, at first, for all writers. That is why professional writers spend years teaching themselves techniques that will help them rediscover their excitement about a story. In this chapter we will learn ways to help students find the overall organic form in their writing and in doing so discover new possibilities for revision.

The Helicopter Ride: Webbing

I've never found prewriting techniques like web-charting very useful before I write, but many students do. (I'm the kind of writer who likes to dive right in. However, after I've dived in, mind mapping helps me to see where I'm going and where I might have gone and could now go. Many writers are compulsive doodlers. In this chapter I'll show you how a little form in your doodling can help your students to find form and direction in their writing after they've written a draft.)

I tell students that web charting is like taking a helicopter ride above a subject. It works well for some students; it doesn't for others. Some students like to web chart before they write in order to find a direction; others, like me, prefer to web chart afterwards as a way of mapping where they've been. Figure 6–1 consists of a high school freshman's web chart of the influences in his life. If he were to freewrite about this topic it would most likely take him much longer to

Figure 6–1   Web Chart

gather all the information. He might even get stuck trying to make a transition from one influence to another. Though the chart may appear general to the outsider, chances are a free-write into any of the strands of the web chart would dig up specific details.

Webbing or clustering can be a great way to make connections faster than you might following sentences across a page. Teach it as a tool for both getting ideas and finding the way when we are lost.

1. Ask students to put their subject in the center of a page. If it's a fiction story they could put the title or simply a main character. If it's an essay then they could put the main thing they're writing about in the middle of the page.

2. This is the nucleus. Have students free-associate ideas in strands off of it. (See Figure 6–1.)

3. Students then look for interesting connections and circle that area. Ask them to write a new lead that grows out of what they circled.

4. Students follow the new lead in a freewrite.

5. After completing a web chart or two, students should ask themselves this one question: "What does the chart tell me about my story and how can I insert, cut, add snapshots, thoughtshots, scenes, and the like, based on what I've learned?"

Moment Mapping

Because fiction stories and personal narratives are made up of moments, sequencing those moments can be a central means for organization and revision. We've already talked about the power of exploding moments and building scenes. Mapping moments can help a student to decide what the big moment is in a story and where it is located in a piece of writing. The following mapping techniques are sometimes used by screen writers and playwrights as they struggle to see how moments fit together.

1. Ask students to read over their story or personal narrative essay. After they've read it, have them make a list, leaving space between each entry, of each moment in the story. Stu-

dents then cut out the moments and shuffle them. (Note: If you use index cards ask students to write one moment per card.)

2. Ask students to arrange the moments in front of them in several different orders. Remind students that as writers they can start in the middle or at the end. Encourage them to take risks.

3. Have students pick one order and glue the moments down.

4. Ask students to make a few notes on revision or questions beside each moment.

5. Have students talk about the process of rearranging moments and how it has changed their story.

Graphing

A graph is a simple table aimed at showing the progress of a character or characters in a particular area. All stories are about people changing. If we graph the life of a character through the story we see a pattern of change. Let's look at a graph of "Cinderella" as an example.

Say we want to show Cinderella's range of emotions in the story. Figure 6–2 illustrates what the graph could look like.

And think of how boring Cinderella's story would be if her path looked like the ones in Figures 6–3 and 6–4.

All stories are about change, and Cinderella's change is mainly in the area of happiness. But don't let the simplicity of this graph deceive you. A student can graph for more than one quality in the same story. He or she can also graph different characters from the same story to see how their lives intersect.

To illustrate, let's graph freedom in the Cinderella story. (See Figure 6–5.) My graph shows that Cinderella is never really free. Sure, she escapes her mean stepsisters, but what would her life be like as a princess? Would she have free reign of the kingdom or would she be expected to toe the royal family line? The end of the story says she lived happily ever after. There is no mention of freedom. It's an issue that the story doesn't deal with because of the time it was written. My graph helps me to see the need for revision if this is a quality I want my character to struggle for.

If I were revising the story of Cinderella for a modern audience, I would try to deal with this issue. My twenty-first-century Cin-

Figure 6–2   Graph of Emotions

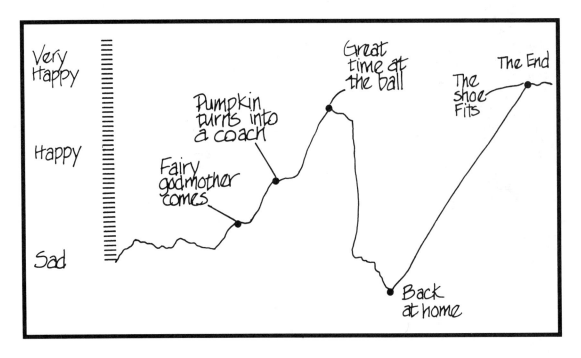

derella might turn down marriage to the Prince in favor of a career as a movie star (unlike Grace Kelly). My revised graph would reflect this (see Figure 6–6). Maybe later she stars in the TV movie of her life and is interviewed by Oprah Winfrey, at which time she reveals why the slipper really didn't fit. My graph of the original story helps me to see new possibilities.

If we were to graph the character of Huck Finn in Mark Twain's novel we might wish to graph Huck's sense of individual moral justice. Huck's adventures on the river with Jim force him to separate his own individual moral conscience from a society that condoned slavery. Our graph might reflect the points in the novel when Huck expresses views contrary to the society he grew up in. We could even turn our graph into a river map heading to an ocean of complete moral understanding. At what points in the book does Huck get closer? When does he slip into backwaters?

Graphing helps us to focus our interest to a particular issue and to see the shape of a story by the terms of that issue.

Figure 6–3   Sad Graph

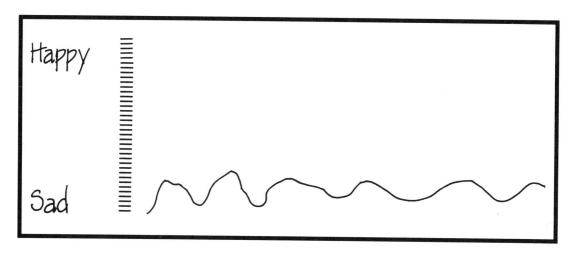

Graphing Characters

1. Before you begin graphing stories with your class, model it several times the way I have above. After you've modeled how to graph a character, ask students to decide on what qualities they wish to graph. It's best to talk about the character's changes in the story and then make the graph about one of these qualities.

2. Students graph a character in a book they are reading. They follow them individually through each chapter of the book, pinpointing moments where change is evident, and make note of techniques the author employs to draw them in at these moments. Ask students: Is there an exploded moment? A big scene? A prolonged thoughtshot?

3. Ask students to graph another character in the story for the same quality, using a different color pen. Note the difference, then have students add a third character with another color pen. Note the relationship between the three.

4. Students write a sentence or two that shows what they learned.

5. Have students graph the main character in one of their

Figure 6–4   Happy Graph

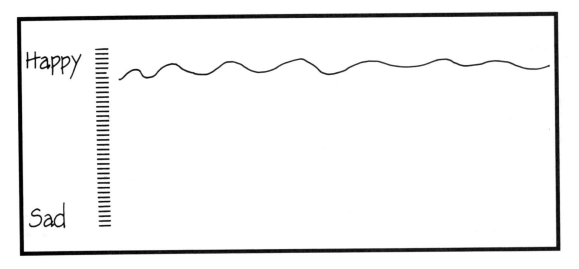

stories. If it's an essay, they can graph the changes in their exploration of their subject. Have them find a moment of change. They then insert either a snapshot, thoughtshot, or scene to make it more important to the reader.

6. Students share the moments of change. Discuss how all stories are about characters changing.

7. After they are comfortable with graphing repeat this process with a story they are currently writing.

Revising the Classics

When Leo Tolstoy found the ending of Shakespeare's *King Lear* to be intolerably sad and unnecessary, he did what any self-respecting arrogant genius would do—he revised it. In Tolstoy's revision neither Cordelia nor King Lear dies. Lear's lesson is learned without the dismal consequences of Shakespeare's tragedy. (It's also interesting to note that Shakespeare himself revised the story according to his own vision. It had previously existed as a folk tale and play, with different plot twists and outcomes.)

British playwright Tom Stoppard was fascinated by the possibility of revising *Hamlet*. His brilliant comedy *Rosencrantz and Guil-*

Figure 6–5   Freedom Graph

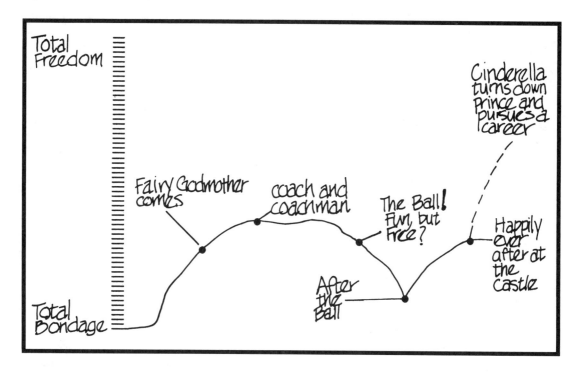

denstern *Are Dead* follows the off-stage lives of two minor characters who are executed in the original play, and in a comic way explores the metaphysical qualities that intrigue us about Hamlet's character.

Revising literature can be a wonderful way to engage students in their reading and make the reading/writing connection in the classroom. Try this exercise to involve students in a piece of classical literature required by your curriculum, or simply to have a good time.

Updated Versions of the Classics

1. Ask students to decide on which qualities to graph characters. Model a few possibilities—some that are in the story already and some that might only apply to a more modern audience. (The earlier discussion about Cinderella is an example.)

2. Students graph a character or characters who interest them.

Figure 6–6   Revised Graph of Modern Cinderella

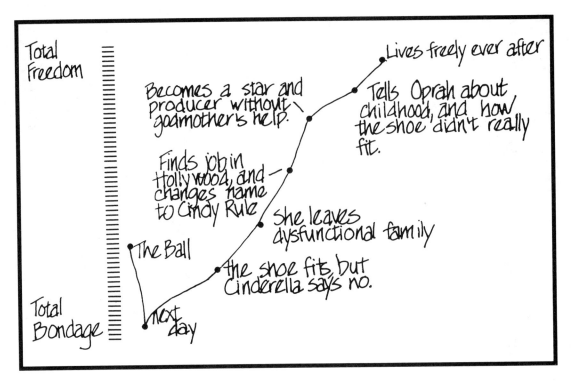

3. Students examine the graph and decide how they could alter that character's path through the story to make it more interesting.

4. Students make a quick outline of their revision.

5. Have students rewrite the scenes or places in question, trying their best to mimic the author's style.

6. Students share their revisions with the class and talk about their process.

Characters Are People Too

I once took a course with a wonderful American literature professor named Gary Lindberg. Gary was an innovative teacher who gave his students alternatives to the analytical literature papers English majors learned to write in their sleep. One assignment was to design a metaphorical map in any way, shape, or form we pleased, and it would serve as a comparison for the nineteenth-century American novels we were studying. The walls of Gary's office were covered with these strange creations, which he said had the advantage of greatly puzzling his colleagues at the university.

For example, one of Gary's students had created a baseball league that equated certain qualities in nineteenth-century American authors' works with baseball skills. One of these qualities was abstinence as control for a pitcher. An author like Henry James, whose books were filled with main characters who renounced their "baser" selves, was a strikeout king on the mound.

For my model, I made five nineteenth-century novelists into surgeons who removed certain qualities from their male and female characters. I created a hermaphrodite figure on a large piece of poster board; it allowed the viewer to see the kind of surgery each novelist performed on both their male and female characters. I had Theodore Dreiser perform a "conscience-ectomy" on his protagonist Sister Carrie but I left in the conscience on his male main character Ralph Hurstwood, who ends up a skid-row bum.

In making the wallet a part of each character's anatomy I was able to show how in the course of a novel characters who lost their conscience fared economically. On the bottom of the poster, I drew a "recovery table" that compared the parts removed by each novelist from each gender.

Gary was delighted with my creation and marveled at some of the connections I was able to make on the recovery table. He honored me by hanging it with the others in his office collection, and he assured me that my chart too would greatly puzzle his colleagues.

Today, when I have forgotten all of the compare/contrast papers I wrote in college, I remember this chart in detail, and I also remember every book I read for that course. Making a map of those characters got me thinking about them as *real* people and they've stuck with me. Inventive strategies can wrench characters out of books and stories and into students' imaginations. Here are a few ways to get students imaginatively re-entering the stories they read and write.

Bringing Characters to Life

- Ask students to conduct an interview with a main character in a story they are reading or writing. Have them ask questions that will get their character to reveal him- or herself beyond what they already know from the story.

• Have students create a scene where characters from two different books meet. They may choose characters who either have something in common or who differ.

• Students can write a letter to a character in a story they're reading or writing. They could ask characters questions and then write a letter back to themselves from the character, or they could ask a classmate to do it. Ask students to record what they learned about the character from their exchange.

• Bring in a video camera to class. Have students act out an interview with a character from a book they're reading or writing.

• Ask students to adapt a book they're reading or writing to a movie screenplay. Ask them to map the story's moments, and then draw pictures for each scene. Explain that film directors call this a storyboard.

• Have students pretend they're a character from a story they're writing. After students explain to the class who they are and what their problem is, the class responds with questions. You could call this a press conference, where characters learn more about themselves by answering others' questions.

Cavewriting

Before we had the alphabet, we drew to communicate with others. Young children also make little distinction between drawing and writing. Unfortunately, we often learn as we get older to value our drawing less. We give it names like "doodling," and unless someone tells us we're artists, we consider our drawing only as a means to relieve boredom or embarrass ourselves. However, drawing pictures, like mind maps, is a powerful way to engage another area of our brains when we write and revise.

I've developed a technique to connect my students with this often untapped resource. It's called cavewriting.

We cavewrite by simply drawing pictures and words to convey such things as emotions, thoughts, and questions. Don't worry if you think you have no drawing talent. That's not the point here. The idea is to get images down on paper and see more than the words themselves.

Here are a few prompts that I've found useful to get students cavewriting.

- Cavewrite the big moment.
- Cavewrite the end of the story.
- Cavewrite the moral of the story.
- Cavewrite the central question.
- Cavewrite a thoughtshot of your main character.
- Cavewrite a snapshot of your main character.
- Cavewrite an explodable moment from your life. Add mini-thoughtshots and snapshots or dialogue to your drawing.

Have students share their cavewrites with each other. Talk about phrases or details they may have added that are not present in their original story. Point out the power of drawing as a tool for seeing more detail in their writing.

The Shape of Things

Many writers talk about the power of visualizing the shape of the pieces they work on. A novel that loops back in time might be shaped like a coiling spiral, an essay centered on one central idea might look like a big duffel bag stuffed with examples. Visualizing the shape of your writing helps you to understand the task at hand for revision. Originally I conceived the chapters of this book as a series of loosely connected boxes, but as it developed I began to see two distinct groups of chapters form together. Now I see the book as two rolling hills with a small valley in between. Like cavewriting, drawing shapes can give writers a handle on where they're going and where they've been.

1. After modeling the process I described above with literature in your classroom or students' own work, ask students to draw the shape of a story they are working on. Tell them there is no right or wrong way to do this. They need only try. (Optional: Try doing this same exercise with modeling clay.)

2. Share shapes and talk about how each story has a different form. Note the similarities also.

In this chapter I've presented several ways to connect students with the organic form of their reading and writing. Whether it's revising the classics or adding snapshots to a story they have written, students become empowered to revise when they see the choices authors have made in writing their stories. Try some of these tools out and experiment with your own creations for helping students see the shape of their writing and reading.

In the last part of this chapter I'll discuss some choices particular to fiction writers.

Spinoffs

- Students graph the characters in their favorite book. Ask them to look for the big moment in their graph and then turn to the corresponding page in the book and observe how the author handles it. Just for fun, encourage students to revise the big moment in their own words. Try experimenting. For example, if the author writes a scene, students write a snapshot of the same moment.
- Have students make a graph or timeline of the story of their life. They then look for the places of the greatest variation and pick one, writing at least one of the following: exploding moment, snapshot, thoughtshot, scene.
- Have students make a web chart for each character in a story they are writing. Ask them to circle areas of interest and note for future reference.
- Ask students to graph every character in a story they are writing for a particular quality or issue that the main character is struggling with.
- Have students pick a story they just plain don't like. They can change the main character so he or she has more of a problem. Or they can write notes about the character, web chart, or just start in by freewriting. If they like what they see, they can try revising the story.
- Have students tell a fairy tale from a different point of view. Ask them to graph each character for a couple of qualities first, and then pick one they're interested in.

● Have everyone revise the ending of a novel, play, or essay the class is reading. Add another chapter or simply rewrite what is there.

First, Second, and Third Person: Fictional Points of View

She is the sunshine of his life.

Stevie Wonder (with point-of-view shift)

Fiction writers have more choices than nonfiction writers. When beginning fiction writers explore form through mapping and graphing, it's crucial that they know about point of view. As teachers we can model these choices for our students through their reading and through demonstration. Once a fiction writer has chosen a point-of-view character, the next decision to make is whether to write the story in the first, second, or third person. It's important to teach students ways to discover the strengths and weaknesses of each point of view.

He/She/They, I/We, or You: How Do You Decide?

Most stories are written in the third or first person, and each has its own distinct advantage.

Third Person (He, She, They) Third person is the most versatile point of view. You can show a character standing by his car in one sentence, and in the next, be inside his mind as he thinks about something that happened ten years ago. You can even describe things that haven't happened yet as well as memories of the past in the same sentence. Look at how Gabriel García Márquez does this in the opening sentence of *One Hundred Years of Solitude*: "Many years later, as he faced the firing squad, Colonel Aureliano Buendia was to remember that distant afternoon when his father took him to discover ice."

The ESP X-Ray Zoom Lens

1. Have students paint a snapshot of a character by simply describing the character rather than calling him or her by name. (Example: "The tall woman with the briefcase entered the building.")

2. Ask students to climb inside the character's head, adding thoughts about some recent problem. ("Darn, can't this elevator move any quicker? thought Carla.")

3. Now have them paint a snapshot of their character up close. ("She wore her best blue wool suit and dangly gold earrings that hung like wind chimes over her shoulders.")

4. They now have another person speak to their main character and have the main character reply in both word and thought. (" 'Oh, Ms. Thompson!' Shirley cried, as she looked at the clock. 'Don't say it, Shirley. I know,' Ms. Thompson interrupted. She hated moments like these, when people felt they had to tell you how late you were, when you knew it already.")

5. Students tell something that's going to happen—something the character doesn't know about yet. ("Carla didn't know it then, but today would be a day she'd remember for the rest of her life.")

This exercise explores some of the major dimensions of a third-person point of view. An author can choose to stay close to one character's thoughts and observations in a story, which is called a third-person limited point of view, or to get into every character's mind and write about everyone's thoughts and observations, which is called an omniscient point of view. (For example, in an omniscient point of view, we'd see what Shirley thought about Ms. Thompson's being late.)

First Person   First person is the most limited point of view. Here, the author stays right inside the character's head and never comes out, and that means the reader has to rely only on what that character believes he or she sees. First-person narrators are their own authors, choosing which thoughts to tell us and which to keep secret. A first-person point of view doesn't allow characters to see themselves, unless they walk in front of a mirror, which is an overused trick, or the author finds some other trick. You can't, for example, say, "My face flushed red and my eyes grew three sizes." How would the character know that?

These are some of the disadvantages of first person. The strength is the sense of intimacy between teller and listener.

I'm Talking to You

1. Have students write a sketch based on the previous exercise from a first-person point of view. ("I am wearing my best blue wool suit, but a lot of good it does me now. I'm late—too late, as usual. I wanted to impress them, but now, with my luck, they'll think I look terrible in blue and my earrings will be the tackiest they've ever seen. They won't care about how I look. They'll just know I'm late.") Point out to students how a story loses some dimension and gains intimacy. A voice is talking to you now, and if that voice is interesting to you, then first person might be a good point of view to use.

2. To help students understand this intimate quality better I sometimes ask them to rewrite first-person love songs and put them into third person. I then ask them what they think is lost and gained.

Second Person   Second person is the least used point of view. Readers don't like to be told they're the main character of a story. It's heavy-handed, like the old commercial that began, "Sure you've got a headache." How many of us told our TV screens that no, we didn't, thank you very much.

It can be an interesting technique, if used very carefully and with great skill, as in Jay McInerney's novel, *Bright Lights, Big City,* which began, "You are not the kind of guy who would be at a place like this at this time of the morning." Some people say that rather than picturing themselves as the main character and becoming irritated, they imagine talking to and looking at the main character through the author's second-person voice when it's used well, as though they, too, know that character, inside and out.

Try rewriting the sketch mentioned previously in the second

person. ("You are wearing your best blue wool suit. You're hoping that your gold dangly earrings remind them of wind chimes and not something tacky, and that's all you can stand to think about right now, because you're late. Too late." Or "You were wearing your best blue wool suit, and you were hoping that your gold dangly earrings reminded them of wind chimes and not something tacky, and that's all you could stand to think about back then, because you were late. Too late.") What do the shifts from present to past tense do to the point of view? Is one easier to read than the other? Is the tone different? How? These are some of the questions you and your students can ponder when thinking about point of view.

Exploring the Angles

I wait until I find a narrative voice. Then I listen to that voice and start writing.

E.L. Doctorow

For the last three years I have been writing and performing original folk songs that retell fairy tales from different points of view. It's been a wonderful exercise in revision because each song requires me to find a new way to imaginatively connect with a story I have heard many times before. In my latest song I retold Cinderella from the fairy godmother's point of view. I have always been fascinated by fairy godmothers and once wrote a children's book called "The Fairy Godmother's Convention." I started by making a list of questions about the story and one jumped out at me: If Cinderella did not live happily ever after, if the Prince ended up divorcing her, would the fairy godmother keep coming back? This question got me my chorus:

I'm a Fairy Godmother
I'm a Fairy God Queen
I'm the best Godmother
You've ever seen
I turn pumpkins to coaches
I turn gerbils to men
and if you're not happy
I come back again.

In writing the song I realized that my fairy godmother could not solve all of Cinderella's problems. The godmother tells Cinderella about the time her Fairy God Husband left her and she turned him into a Fairy God Toad. It didn't solve a thing. It just made her feel bad when she found him a year later flattened on a road. In the last verse my godmother gives Cinderella the bottom line.

My dear Cinderella, what can I say,
I wish there was something I could do for you right away
but you know fairies do magic and people do work,
the next time you marry, don't marry a jerk!

Finding new points of view on old stories is a wonderful way to reclaim our excitement in any subject and learn what stories really mean to us. Here's an exercise I did with a seventh-grade social studies class that was studying the Revolutionary War.

A People's History of the World

After reading several books on history or historical fiction about the period and studying the historical events of the day with your class, read and share with your class Howard Zinn's book, *The People's History of the United States.* (New York: Harper & Row, 1980). Zinn makes a very cogent point. History as we know it is told from the point of view of the oppressors. For example, we learned in school that Columbus was a great man for discovering what we today call America. But what would Columbus look like from the Arawak Indians' point of view? Many historians say there was a small population of Indians on the islands Columbus discovered. In reality, that small population consisted of three-and-a-half million men, women, and children, compared to the fifty men on Columbus's boat. Within the first two years most of the Arawaks perished from disease, and the remaining few who weren't murdered were forced into a life of slavery. It's no wonder that Native Americans everywhere are protesting the celebrations that are occuring in 1992 to mark the 500th anniversary of Columbus's maiden voyage. Would the French want to celebrate Hitler's invasion of France?

Tell your students if we want history to be more than "his story," we need to look at it from many different points of view.

1. Have your students brainstorm of lists of possible points of view for a story about your time period—in this case, The Revolutionary War.

Here are a few my class came up with:

- British spy
- French person
- Front-line Colonial soldier
- African slave
- Minister at a hanging of a traitor
- Farmers
- Teenage girl who saw Benedict Arnold pass documents to the British
- Doctor on the war front
- Native Americans
- Soldier's brother or sister
- King George
- Nathan Hale's hangman
- Eight-year-old drummer boy

2. Working in small groups, each student picks a character and brainstorms or web-charts about that character's life. Remind students to give their character a problem and give him or her relationships with other people.

3. Have students question conference with each other or conduct a press conference where that character takes questions from the whole class.

4. Students then turn the most compelling questions into leads, and begin writing their stories. (This exercise could work with students writing in pairs. Students could create two characters from the same story and write the story collaboratively.)

5. Share stories and ask the authors to write about what they learned about history through the eyes of the character they imagined. Post some of these stories on a bulletin board with the narratives of what students learned beside the stories.

Give it a title like, "The People's View of the Revolutionary War."

Inexperienced writers don't enjoy revision for the same reason some students get bored with school. They don't see the imaginative possibilities. Mapping and graphing stories and playing with points of view help students to not only discover form, but to understand the range of imaginative promise at their disposal.

Spinoffs

- Ask students to find a book written in the third person and rewrite several paragraphs in the first person. Observe the difference.

- Have students find a book written in the first person and rewrite the first two paragraphs in the third person. Try exploring different dimensions that you couldn't do in the first person. Also have students write in the plural first and plural third person ("we" and "they") to discover more dimensions.

- Ask students to write about waking up in the morning from the second-person point of view, trying to include any comic elements they can think of.

- Ask students to write a scene in the third person or find one in their writing folders. Have them insert several snapshots and thoughtshots into the scene. Then have them revise the scene to first person, editing the snapshots. Discuss the differences in the point of view.

- Have students experiment rewriting the lyrics to songs in all three persons. ("Your country 'tis of thee..")

- Have students look up the word *woman* in an old World Book Encyclopedia (1968–1972). After reading the definition about the varied roles women play in society, have them look up *man*. (There is usually no definition for man or men, but simply a note that says: "See *human being*"). Ask students how this could be. Ask them whose point of view wrote the encyclopedia. Ask them to write a definition for *man* or *men*.

They can write it from any point of view they choose: women's, extraterrestrials, dogs, cats, anything they choose, only they must not reveal the point of view in their entry. Share definitions and have the class guess whose point of view has written them. Discuss the importance of reading between the lines when examining any source, even the "holy" encyclopedia.

• Have students pretend they are extraterrestrials. They have just landed on Earth and must send reports back home. Ask students to create their own or choose one of these phenemena to report back home about:

A bowling alley

A man smoking a cigarette

Children playing with dolls

People playing baseball

Don't Fix My Story, Just Listen to Me

A Guide to Conferencing and Codependency

*I think I did pretty well considering I started out
with a bunch of blank paper.*
Steve Martin

It's 10:00 A.M., time to conference with Jane, and you haven't even read her seventeen-page story about a blind date. You are a terrible teacher, a lazy teacher, a teacher who should no doubt be denied recertification. You shouldn't have gone out last night for that fried clam dinner, even though it was nice to spend some time with your family. That was not fair to Jane. You also blew your diet, which proves you have no willpower and are therefore a terrible role model for the kids. Sleeping last night was also a selfish thing to do. You had stories to read, work to correct, and you chose to drift off into your own unconscious, self-absorbed dream world. What kind of a teacher are you, anyway?

There's Jane sitting across from you. Innocent Jane with the big brown eyes and beautiful smile. Jane, who writes those lovely long stories that you, slug teacher that you are, move to the bottom of the pile only because they are the thickest.

"So Jane, tell me what you changed in the story."

Jane points out an exploded moment she added on page eleven. It's the moment when Shawn approaches Claire's house. She tells you she really wanted you to feel what Sean felt approaching the fancy house. You read it, and it works much better.

"Very dramatic. Good job," you tell her.

Next she points out the snapshot she inserted on page five of Sean's beat-up 1976 Chevy Nova. She tells you she wanted the reader to get a mental image of how poor Shawn was without actually telling you.

"Wonderful, Jane," you say as you read it for the first time. "I love that detail about the torn vinyl seat. It makes the whole snapshot come alive."

"I also built a scene at the moment when he wants to kiss her. I wanted to have him not know what to say, so I had him talk about the Red Sox and she pretends to be interested."

"Yes, I like it," you say. "Maybe you could even insert some of his thoughts there so the reader can feel how he feels stupid."

Jane takes note of your suggestion and is eager to work more on that scene. She is excited that you liked her additions to her story and could praise them specifically. She thanks you for the conference.

You think you are a phony, but in reality you have actually done an excellent job at conferencing with Jane. You let her control the direction of the conference. You responded to her work as an interested reader, not a teacher-corrector, and you have given her a simple suggestion that has filled her with a desire to work more on her story. If you had spent an hour last night reading her story, you no doubt would have a page full of suggestions for improving her story. You would have told her to add more detail in her early snapshots of Sean. You would have told her to cut some of that early dialogue that seemed unnecessary. You may have even suggested that she explode a different moment in the story and add thoughtshots of Sean throughout. If you had only spent more time you could have told Jane exactly how to revise her story, and she would have walked away from the conference with a page of notes and a feeling that she needed to write more to please you. Aren't you glad you are a lazy slug teacher?

I'm not advocating that teachers shouldn't prepare for their classes; rather, I want to show you ways of teaching that will help teach your students to be their own editors and not depend on you to do the most important work for them.

Jane may seem like an ideal student who doesn't need much prodding, but Matt is different and he is next. He's written two sentences and wants you to "help" him. You know you could spend an hour with him brainstorming new ideas but there are five more students lined up behind. What are you going to do?

When some teachers tell me how impossible it is to conference with each student each week, I immediately know they see conferences as a way of fixing their students' work, and they won't have effective conferences until in some essential way they revise their relationship with their students and themselves. In this chapter I'll show you ways to create a relationship with your students that puts them in charge.

The Absentee Conference

1. Tell students that instead of a conference you want them to write a dialogue between you and them talking about your paper. This can be like a play and they don't have to be realistic if they don't want to be. Let their imaginations have a free rein.

2. Have them bring the script to the next conference and read it or even act it out together.

3. Discuss the dominant theme of the script and ask them what is the most helpful thing you do for them in a conference.

The first time I tried this exercise was with college freshmen. I am a very liberal-minded teacher who encourages experimentation and talks often and openly about students taking risks. I insisted that my conferences be student-directed and tried to keep my mouth shut whenever humanly possible. It was very surprising to me that several of my students viewed me as a mad scientist who gleefully dissected their weekly writing as they looked on in horror. Part of the problem was in their perception of the generic teacher, which they had learned through school, but I also had to look at my relationship with them in light of this perception, and I hadn't been doing that before. I had assumed that the image they were receiving was the image I was projecting. This was a false assumption.

Before we can revise our relationship with our students, however, we need to understand it. Recently, I went into a school where much of the instruction was traditional, basal-oriented. Almost every teacher complained that their students had a hard time being creative. They were impressed by my work and amazed at the stories their children wrote under my simple instruction. One teacher said she once had an effective method of getting her children to create. She shut off all the lights, lit candles, and dressed up as a witch. "I give you the power of creativity," she would utter to them as she sprinkled flash powder at the candle flame. Though it was against the school's fire regulations, and she was eventually asked to stop by the principal, she informed me that it did work. The only trouble was that one of her students cried and refused to write the next year when his fifth-grade teacher refused to put on a witch costume and shut off the lights.

This teacher's story is a perfect example of what pop psychologists would call codependent behavior. The teacher sees herself as an enabler who allows her children to learn through her sacred curriculum. Even something as individualistic as creativity must be granted by the all-powerful high priestess. Ironically, this teacher did not see herself as a dominating figure in the class. Rather, she saw the class as timid, dull children who were afraid to take risks without her permission. If teachers don't hand down responsibility and choice to their students, they end up carrying it for everybody, and what a burden it is. No wonder these teachers are afraid of collaborative learning environments, where children are encouraged to make choices. If I am personally responsible for every choice a student makes in my classroom, how can I possibly let them make more than a few choices?

Here is part of a group writing conference in a classroom where whole language has been successful. One of the people in this conference is the teacher. Can you tell who?

Kelly: Do you think I should leave in the description of the bedroom?

Sarah: If you don't know anything about where they live it could be a poor person who lives in a one-room apartment building instead of the mansion it is.

Kelly: Ben told me I should leave it in there.

Ben: Read the beginning again.

Kelly: (reads) "Hi. My name is Lorna, I live in the Dakota Apartment building. It's one of the richest apartment buildings in New York City." You see, that's where I get the idea that they are rich.

Ben: Well you know my mother lived in a real fancy apartment building but they lived in a really small apartment. One bedroom for the five of them. We had a kitchen, a living room, and a bathroom. It's hard to tell. You might want to put something else to show she's rich.

Jane: You could say something like, "As she walked up to the apartment and saw a homeless man walking down the street, she realized how lucky she was to live in a big apartment that had three rooms for herself while all these people who lived on the streets didn't even have one room."

Judy: I kinda think its important too because it shows they have servants and that the servants are upper-class.

The teacher's are Ben and Judy and Jane and Kelly. They are all fourth graders. This was a peer conference. This is how it should be. This is how it *must* be for conferences to be successful. One way to encourage this type of student-centered initiative is to have students contract daily with you to define their course of action and to know what to expect from each other and from you. Teachers often ask me, "What if a kid decides not to write during his writing period? What do I do? He tells me he's not inspired." My reply is simple. "What would you do if you handed him a worksheet to do and he gave you the same response?" Chances are there would be some consequence. The same should be true for a wasted writing period, especially since there could be dozens of activities to choose from. However, to create an effective structure for a writing period the children need to own it, create it, and agree to it as a group; otherwise, you are promoting a top-down model that will work against your goals. Here's one way of doing it.

Structuring Writing Time

1. With the entire class, brainstorm a list of all the activities you could do during a writing period. Things like webbing; freewriting; writing snapshots, thoughtshots, scenes; and illustrating are some you might want to list.

2. Edit the list as a group and refine it. Post it somewhere in the classroom for reference.

3. Ask students to contract each day for what they are going to do in writing period. Make a form that works for you. Here's what I like to do.

Goal: To work on my grandmother story
Action: list details, freewrite snapshots
Result: found some good memories of my grandfather I'd forgotten. I think I want to write about him now.

4. If students are stuck, refer them to the list. Chances are they will get unstuck soon. If students bring their contracts to conference, they can refer to them and have a place to begin talking about their work.

Questions on Paper: Keeping the Edge in Peer Conferences

Peer conferencing is a central element of a student-centered classroom. The more you empower your students, the less they will have to line up at your desk for a conference. However, many teachers have had poor luck with peer conferencing. They talk about students who don't ask evocative questions and disorganized classrooms where conference time is wasted chit-chatting. Here are a couple of ideas to make peer conferences more accountable and to model important conference skills for your students.

1. Create a form for your students to use for each conference they have. The form could be as simple as a piece of paper with the date and the students' names. One idea would be to have three headings on the sheet of paper: Questions the Reader wants to know more about, Comments, and Concerns. Another way would be to simply write:

- I like:
- I wonder:
- Questions:
- Plan for action:

The writer fills out the last section at the end of the peer conference when his or her partner's comments are still fresh.

2. On an overhead projector with a full class workshop, model how to use the form with one student's work. Teach students to ask questions and make specific comments (see Chapter 1). Teach them to abbreviate their comments so they can say the most in the shortest amount of time. Model this many times for your class so they will understand the importance of the peer conference.

3. Each time a student has a peer conference, he or she must fill out one of these forms, and it is then stapled to the top of the conferee's story for future reference. This record of the conference will help make your students more accountable to you for their conference time, and before long you may find the line at your own desk diminishing.

The Internal Critic

Students walking away from a conference are frequently overwhelmed with information. It's important to teach them to learn how to listen to their own internal critics, which can sift through the comments and questions of their peers or teacher and find what's important for revision. In all conferences some questions or comments will make students want to add more to their work; others won't mean a thing. Tell students that the best time to listen to their internal critic is directly after the conference. Ask them to spend a few minutes jotting down revision plans in their plan-for-action section on the conference sheet.

The Status of the Class

In the old days a teacher gave one assignment and the class responded by doing it that day. Organization was simple. But how do you organize a class where everybody is working on different writing projects? Here's a straightforward way to keep tabs on all your students' writing:

- Create a chart like the one in Figure 7–1.

- Create a series of initials that refer to the stages of the writing process as defined by your class. Don't be afraid to deviate from standard forms. For example, you may want to have a stage called "Inserting" (snapshots, thoughtshots, scenes) and initial it "I".

- Either through daily contract or through oral check find out where each student is at each writing period. This way you will know to nudge the student who has been editing a story for a week.

Sarah was a seventh-grade teacher who put her hand up after lunchtime at a writing course I taught for teachers this summer.

"I'm confused," she began, and went on to ask some particular questions. It was a typical assignment-oriented question. My first reaction, as teacher, was to take responsibility for her confusion. I must not have been clear, I thought. I never seem to say things clearly enough. That's my problem. I began to explain to her the assignment, but my explanation wasn't really making things clearer. I am such a terrible organizer, I thought. I take after my mother. But then, was it me, or was it her? All the other students seemed to get it. Why didn't she? Was Sarah listening when I gave the assignment? Finally, as she continued to voice her confusion I realized what had gone wrong. I had been suckered into being the enabler. I knew at that moment exactly what to say.

"Tell me which way of doing the assignment will help you to learn the most."

She told me and I simply approved and commended her ability to understand her own learning process. Then I turned to the rest of the class of teachers and said, "See, that's how you hand over a choice. Wasn't that easy?"

Figure 7–1   Status-of-the-Class Chart

name	Monday	Tuesday	Wednesday	Thurs.	Friday
Jessie	IG old days	no writing	R old days	D old days	PC Picasso RP
Kenny	LW snake	N W	R snake	LW snake	PC Grandpa
Fiona	E Bookr		E Bookr	IG story	D trip s
Kaitlin	I Poem Cats		EP Cats	IG poem	EX Mother
Kurt	E car essay		D car essay	M car essay	PC Renoir
Sarah	R Horse RP		LW Horse	D Horse	IG poem
Sophie	R Monet P		I Monet	LW Monet	IG Story
Wallace	IG poem		LW P. Death	I Death	IG Story
Gavin	E poem Fences		E poem Fences	IG story	LW The Fires
Leila	RP IG weaving		LW RP Weaving	R weaving	D weaving
Leslie	PC God Poem		I God Poem	I God	IG poem
Steven	PC Dairy Farming	↓	IG no idea	LW poem Hope	I poem Hope

Codes

IG = Idea gathering
LW = Lead Writing
I = Inserting (snapshots, thoughtshots)

E = Editing
PC = Peer conf.
EX = Exploding a moment
M = Mapping
R = Researching

D = Drafting   NW = No Writing

Spinoffs

Conferencing is a technique for helping writers make choices and define direction. All teachers need to learn better ways to encourage this process and as they do, their work becomes easier in some very essential ways. What follows are some simple guidelines to try out when and if you find yourself bogged down with conferences.

• Always make sure the student speaks first. Train students to come to conferences with either a short paragraph about their story, a list of questions, or their most recent contracts, which can be a record of their process with the piece. Your first job is to get them talking.

• Resist the desire to fix a student's story, especially if you have brilliant advice. The final product may turn out better, but the student will lose ownership of the story if you are not careful. If you have some good ideas, ask a few questions to get the student thinking in that direction. Who knows? He or she may come up with a better idea than the one you had.

• Whenever you or your students feel bogged down with the writing on the paper, simply put it aside and talk about the writing off the page. For example, a student has written a story about his grandmother and told in it how she baked apple pies. You can spend the conference talking about apple pies or you can ask him to tell you some other things he did with his grandmother. Chances are, the more he thinks about all the stuff he left out about his grandmother, the closer he'll get to his purpose for writing.

• Take notes as your student talks. In talking about a subject kids sometimes find great leads or find a new focus. If no one takes notes they can get lost. It's also a great way to keep the kids in control. Your notes don't have to be (and shouldn't be) advice. Rather, let them be an accurate reflection of what your students said. You can turn to them near the end of a conference and say, "This is what you said."

• Vary the style of a conference when you feel as if you're getting in a rut. Here are some suggestions:

• Work with two or three students at a time. This can be a great help because you'll be able to deflect your need to fix things by turning to another child and saying, "What do you think?"

- Ask students to conference one-on-one with each other first, then meet with you to discuss the issues that came up in their conference. This way your thoughts are relegated to the realm of second opinion.
- Design conferences around themes—leads, editing, organization, idea getting. Defining a focus in advance helps students to sharpen their intentions when they come to conference.

- Limit your directions to one and ask the student to define it, like this: "So where are you going now with this story?" If you give a suggestion, let it come after a student has at least tried to define a direction. She may surprise you and say exactly what you were going to or even something more important to her. Best of all she will *own* it.

- Respond to a student's writing as a reader—not as a teacher. An honest reader response tells a writer the effect of his words and lets him begin to think about how to rearrange them. A teacher's response directs from the start and shortchanges the student of his own invaluable perceptions and personal ownership of his work.

- Tape-record conferences for your own benefit. Listen to your role and think about how you could do it better.

- Have faith in the process when things are tough. Realize that every conference won't be perfect and that above all you don't have to fix a student's paper in the name of productivity. If students say they don't want to write, it's not your job to make them creative. You can ask questions, you can suggest directions, but they must make the final choices. Better to have a directionless conference where the student is in control than a focused conference where you have defined the direction. The first could get the student looking for direction, the second will get the student following orders.

- Break these guidelines whenever you want to. Dare to make mistakes and take risks. For example, sometimes a gentle suggestion at the right time will save a student weeks of meandering. Trust your instincts and develop them.

Of Masters and Monkeys: Creating a Writing Salon in the Classroom

Students in whole-language classrooms learn to read with writers' eyes, seeing not only the traditional content of a piece but how the writer achieved his or her goals. I can always tell when I'm in such a classroom, because when I question a student on an idea I'll hear comments like, "I want to do an ending like Tomie DePaola," or "I want to develop a character like Beverly Cleary does it." For years writers, and all artists for that matter, have done the same thing. Renoir was influenced by Monet. Hemingway was influenced by Dostoyevsky. Alice Walker claims Zora Neale Hurston as her mentor. No artist creates in a vacuum. Like children separating themselves from parents to discover their own unique personalities, artists wean themselves from the powerful influences who both inspired them to create and showed them the way. It's a long process, often taking years. In medieval times it was called an apprenticeship, and still is in certain crafts today.

If we think of our students and ourselves as apprentice writers and the Louisa May Alcotts and Jack Londons as the blackbelt masters, then we begin to develop a classroom that more closely resembles the artist's studio.

All writers have influences that become textbooks on writing they carry in their heads. For students in the middle grades it might look something like this:

Chapter one: Make up a place like Terabithia.

Chapter two: Make up a kid who no one likes but has some magic thing like James in *James and the Giant Peach.*

Chapter three: Make up an adventure story like *Hatchet.*

Like Gertrude Stein, to whose salon in Paris all the great writers of the time flocked, teachers must acknowledge the many different genres of writing and provide the light and space for them to flourish. Create a salon in your classroom where artists from different genres feed off one another's art.

Here are a few suggestions.

Create the Atmosphere   Find ways of deinstitutionalizing the classroom. Put a rug down, create a Parisian cafe complete with hot chocolate in one corner, or simply get a couple of old sofas— anything you can do to alter the academic atmosphere will enhance your writers' ability to create. If you think this is a silly and un-necessary pretense answer this question: How many great works of Western literature were written in school?

Reading/Writing Conferences   A reading conference can follow the same format as a writer's conference. It is an opportunity for readers to share their insights and feelings about a book that they are reading. (They work well with small groups.) We can apply the same model I discussed in chapter 3 to reading (see pages 41–43). When we read we plunge into the text and let ourselves get swept away by what the story tells us. But the moment someone walks up to us and asks, "Read any good books lately?" we im-mediately start to climb the mountain and look at the patterns on the waves. "Yes. I read this great book by Roald Dahl called *Matilda*. It was about a schoolgirl in a mean school."

A teacher's job is to get students to examine and clarify their perceptions and also to respond as any other curious fellow reader might. "What did you like about it? What was the school like? I read an adult book like that once. It was called *The Young Toreless*, by an early twentieth-century German writer named Robert Musil."

To understand why a book is boring or exciting for you is central to the literate experience, and the first step in making the con-nection between what you read and what you write. Once students start questioning their responses they immediately begin examining aspects of craft. For example, "The book was boring because there was not enough description."

Ask students to keep a running log of questions as they read and bring them to the reading conference.

Jane Hansen has explored reading conferences in depth in her book *When Writers Read*.

Reading/Writing Journals   When writers read they have the same experience film directors have when they watch a movie or chefs when they sit down to eat in a restaurant or composers when they listen to a symphony. They are not simply passive absorbers of story, characters, plots—they are scavengers looking for new ideas, reviewers intrigued by or skeptical of a clever plot, writers anxious to try out that new ending in their *own* story.

A reading journal gives readers a chance to climb the mountain and explore their perceptions. The format is simple: the student writes a letter to the teacher and the teacher writes a letter back to the student. (Nancie Atwell's *In the Middle* contains wonderful examples of reading journals.) As a class it's a good idea to brain-storm a list of questions you can ask each other in these letters. This way the writers who need it will be able to refer to this list as a way to prod their pens into action.

Here is an excerpt from a reading journal between Deborah Craig, a teacher at Stratham Memorial School, and her student Josh. Notice how the questions keep the exchange alive.

Dear Josh,

I am reading a bunch of books on philosophy and religion. I am skipping between books and making some comparisons.

I like the question you chose to answer. I would like to ask you the same questions you ask the author. You are a writer. Where do you get your ideas for books? Have you ever thought about writing a "choose your own adventure"?

Love,
Ms. Craig

Dear Ms. Craig,

Yes, I did think about wrighting a "choose your own adventure" but they seemed too hard. I get my ideas for books by things that happen or books that kids write. I finished *Lost on the Amazon* by R.A. Montgomery and *Ghost Hunter* by Edward Packards. I'm read-ing *Dear Mr. Henshaw* by Beverly Cleary. My question is What's your favorite character. My favorite carector is Leigh Boots. I'm only on the second page so far.

Josh

Dear Josh,

Brandon is also reading *Dear Mr. Henshaw* so you might want to get together with him and talk about it. He's a little confused about what's happening in the book and maybe you can help him.

I have a lot of favorite characters. I think if I had to pick my most favorite, it would be Max from *Where the Wild Things Are*. I like his character and I like his wolf suit.

I think saying it's too hard to write a "choose your own adven-ture" is a cop out. I think you should think about what the most important thing is to make a "choose your own adventure" book work.

What do you think the real reason is for Leigh writing to Mr. Henshaw?

Love,
Ms. Craig

Dear Ms. Craig,
I think the thing about wrighting a "choose your own adventure" is having it make sense.
No I'v never thought of how to wright one.
I'm still reading *Dear Mr. Henshaw*. I'm on 125-almost done. I think the story is about Leigh dealing with his parents devorse. Like when Leigh is sad I'm sort of sad, well this is a hard book to explane.

Josh

It's easy to see the reading-writing connection in these journal entries. Ms. Craig not only responds to questions about reading, she suggests a writing topic and refers Josh to another student who might benefit from his insight into the book he's reading. Reading can be one of the best ways of getting inspired. The next time a student tells you he or she doesn't know what to write about, suggest a conference with Roald Dahl or S. E. Hinton or Lois Duncan. Tell students that all writers have dry spells and nudge them to explore different genres.

Spinoffs

- Regularly ask students to swap reading journals, between each other and even other classes in the school.
- Develop a list of questions with your students that they can refer to when they are stuck writing in their reading journal. Hang them in the classroom as a reference.
- If you don't have time to write in each student's journal each week, try writing a letter to your entire class, telling students what you've been reading and inviting some sort of response. Hand them the letter and give them thirty minutes or more to write a response. Read their responses and respond to them as a whole the next week, perhaps singling out one or two provocative questions to answer. This is a great way to model your own literacy and can allow you more time to genuinely explore your own reading and model that exploration to your class.
- Occasionally, read literature from a writer's point of view.

Illustrate a wonderful exploded moment or act out a powerful scene, as we did in chapter 4. Turn to students and say, "Wow, look how Katherine Paterson or Gary Paulsen did that. Isn't that something!"

• The best way to empower your students is to get their ideas and work on the walls of your classroom. Whether it's lists of writing activities or favorite leads from books students have read, find ways to involve your class in interior decoration.

• Have regular formal or informal sharing sessions where students share their work without any critical response. Teach the audience to listen and applaud after each reading. When possible, expand your students' audience beyond the classroom. Display work in other parts of the school or get the local newspaper to publish work.

• When possible, find ways to interact with other classes. Whether it's putting on plays for the younger grades or reading or making instructional videos for older students, the best way to create purpose in student writing is to expand the audience.

• A literary tea or a writer's lunch, where students share their work, can be a wonderful way to generate excitement about writing. It's so simple, but it works!

• Parents' nights at schools can often be uneventful affairs where parents come to see how their kids are "doing." Why not make a parents' evening that will help parents learn what their children are learning? Some of the most inspiring workshops I have ever conducted have had students and their parents writing side by side. Try designing an evening that is part student reading and part writing workshop for students and parents.

• Start a corkboard of quotes from published writers, both from your class and the larger literary world. Tell students to refer to these quotes for advice and encouragement. Add more and more quotes from your students to the board.

Re-entering a Draft

*I learned the need to disrespect the typewritten page,
even to take satisfaction in plowing up those neat rows
of words with a pencil if they didn't seem to serve
my purpose.*

Bruce Ballenger

A student who knows a language of craft and has successful conferences can still have trouble finding a doorway back into a draft. In this chapter I'll show you practical tips to help students re-enter their writing and ways to foster your role as helpful editor.

Space: The Necessary Frontier

I like to leave out the parts readers skip over.

Elmore Leonard

There are certain laws of physics that apply to revising what is on the page. The tighter the molecular structure, the harder it is to penetrate; the looser, the easier. It's easier to cut through butter than steel. The same applies to writing. Large, tangled, paragraph-less chunks of writing with no space are harder to penetrate and rearrange than double-spaced writing that gives the reader/editor a place to rest eyes and fill that space with thoughts. This book has big margins for you to write in, and my editor insisted that I double-space the original manuscript and only write on one side of the paper so she could read it more easily and insert her comments and questions exactly where they occurred. Any graphic designer will tell you that space allows a reader to enter a piece of writing.

In this chapter I offer a few techniques to help students make space for readers and editors in their stories. (Note: Revision on a computer makes some of these techniques less important or much easier, but until the day when all students have daily access to their own computer, handwritten revision will always be essential. Students who wait for computer time to revise will miss out on much of the important flexibility that playing with rough drafts can add to their writing.)

Making Space

Double-Spacing

Yes, I know it wastes trees because more paper gets used, so you may not want to have students do this all the time, but double-spacing can be the best way of teaching revision.

Try having students exchange their double-spaced stories with a partner. As they read one another's stories they are expected to write down questions in between the lines exactly where they come up.

These questions become a guide for revision. A question like What did he look like? can suggest adding a snapshot. Students can turn some questions into new leads for the piece. (Note: Students should also only write on one side of the paper in case they decide to cut and paste.)

Chapters: Attacking Long Stories

"What do I do when they write these stories that go on and on and on?" This is the lament I hear from many teachers in the middle grades. Faced with a fifteen-page story students view the task of revision as daunting. Good editors faced with the same problem would know what to do. They would ask the writer to put the story into chapters or sections. A chapter is like a paragraph. It defines a piece of the story, gives emphasis, and provides the writer with an effortless way to make major transitions.

How do we break a long story into chapters? Here are some basic suggestions to pass on to your students. There are many other possibilities.

- When a new day is beginning.
- When the story switches to a different point-of-view character.
- When something dramatic is about to happen.
- When you want a lot of time to pass but don't want to write about it (e.g., Chapter one: 1941; Chapter two: 1987).
- When you want to switch gears in any major way (e.g., Chapter one: the murder; Chapter two: The detective getting a phone call as he sips ginger ale on the French Riviera).

Pictures and Pages

Picture books are usually made up of chunks of text arranged around illustrations, and they can help older students make sense of transitions in writing. Paging up text and making illustrations are a wonderful way to get space into a story. Here's a technique I've found successful.

1. Show students a picture book and describe how illustrators find pictures in stories. Ask them to find five or ten pictures in their story and put a check in the margin at those places.

2. Have students chunk up their story into pages, using their check marks as a guide. This can be done with scissors if they have written on one side of the paper in the original. In that case they would glue their page onto a new sheet of paper leaving room for revision. Otherwise students can copy each chunk onto a single sheet of paper.

3. Students shuffle the pages and swap one or two with a partner. Ask students to write two questions that will help their partner revise. Have them keep swapping until all the pages have been seen.

4. Using your questions revise one or two pages, adding more detail, snapshots, thoughtshots, scenes, and whatever else makes sense.

Paragraphs and White Space

Paragraphing is another way to make space. Traditionally, paragraphing was taught to students as a simple formula: topic sentence and supporting ideas. There is nothing wrong with this formula other than the fact that it is a formula and can give kids a constricted idea of what a paragraph is. I would opt for a way to teach paragraphing that is closer to how kids write. In other words, there are some who write excellent transitions and topic sentences before they even start indenting them and calling them paragraphs. These students don't need to learn how to write paragraphs but rather how to identify ones they have already written.

Give students a few simple guidelines and see how well they can paragraph without the formula. I think you'll be surprised.

- A paragraph is when one thing shifts to another thing—a shift in thought, a movement in a story, a change in point of view, or a change in speaker.
- A paragraph is a new idea or a shift in direction.
- A paragraph is when a new person is speaking.

- A paragraph is like a giant period at the end of a clump of sentences. End one at a dramatic place for more effect. The last sentence of a paragraph has more impact than the sentences before.
- A paragraph is where the writer wants to create space in the reader's mind. Experiment and try making paragraphs where you want the reader to pause.

Pablo Casals once said that music is the spaces between the notes. In some ways the same is true of literature. It is the spaces between words and sentences that define the reader's response. As students learn to create space in their work they are simultaneously gaining an awareness of audience, which will help them begin to see the power of their words.

Spinoffs

- Students cut up a story into paragraphs or sentences, then shuffle them and keep the ones they like. Have them rewrite the story by pasting what they saved on a new piece of paper.
- Students take a piece of published writing and reparagraph it. Discuss the effect it has to make short paragraphs longer and vice versa.
- Read a published book to the class and discuss the reasons why an author breaks chapters in certain places.
- Have students read a children's picture book and see if they can find some good illustrations the illustrator did not see. Ask kids to draw them.

Editors, Not Teachers: Writing on Student Papers

It's my experience that very few writers, young or old, are really seeking advice when they give their work to be read. They want support; they want someone to say, "Good job."

John Irving

Many writing-process teachers I've talked to pride themselves on the fact that they never write on student papers. They don't want to take anything away from the student, and they know that even helpful comments can come across as meaningless when written down on paper. They remember all the "Awks," "Word Choices," and other pithy remarks their grammarnoic teachers sprawled in red ink over their papers. They know the power of a teacher's pen and the importance of conferencing with their students to get the rest of the story. Commenting in writing tends to solidify work on the page, whereas conferencing is a way of probing the unwritten text.

Though I share these concerns, I also know from my own work with good editors and teachers that I've gained invaluable knowledge from their scribbling on my work. Good editors make notes to themselves, as a reader would marking up a textbook. Sharing with the writer these notes, usually written on post-its or in pencil, is a way of closely monitoring a reading. The post-it can be removed during the conference or saved by the student for future reference. The pencil can be erased.

Students can also use post-its to mark places of confusion or interest when reading one another's papers or books. When students and teacher have a shared language, writing on papers becomes less threatening, especially when a teacher has structured a classroom as a community of writers.

We can teach students a few guidelines for writing on papers that will help them to respect one another's work and offer constructive criticism. This chapter will give you some ideas for structuring written criticism offered in the classroom.

Praise Is the Glue

▬▬▬▬▬▬ Dear Billy,

I loved your story. It's really exciting and fun and great to read. You are a terrific writer. It's so much fun to read the stories you write. What a great job you did on this one!

　　Ms. Jones

At first glance this is a very encouraging letter that any writer would be happy to receive. It's full of praise and encouragement, and it would certainly make the reader feel good about him- or herself and the job he or she is doing. But just for a minute let's pretend we are Billy and see what he might take away from this letter.

Billy's thoughts: Gee, Ms. Jones really liked my story. She thinks I'm a great writer. Boy it was lucky I thought up that idea about the flying mouse. That was an exciting story because of that. I better think up something like that for the next story, too. Don't want to disappoint Ms. Jones.

Because Ms. Jones praises Billy and not specific qualities in his writing, Billy must make his own guess as to why she liked his story. Ms. Jones's blanket approval, like a critic's unqualified praise, is seen as something Billy could lose if he doesn't write his next story in the same way. Suppose instead Ms. Jones had said, "I love the way you always use your imagination to find new ideas. It's great to see how much you enjoy playing with characters." Then she would be giving Billy permission to play more instead of implying he had found a formula to repeat.

As a rule, criticism can easily backfire if it is couched in terms of approval or disapproval. The moment a teacher says something like "That's good," every student in the class begins to wonder if what they wrote was good, too. It would be better if the teacher said nothing at all or could specifically praise the quality in the writing that makes it good. "Gee, I love that detail about the cold sweat on the back of his neck. It really makes me feel like I'm right there with you." A comment like this focuses the students on the craft of writing, not on the teacher's approval. If this teacher continues to praise the use of detail, she will quickly find her students writing with more and more detail.

Praising specifically is something that takes practice. Here's an exercise to help.

Praising Specifically

1. Write a letter of specific praise to the best writer in your class. Now write one to the weakest writer. Don't say anything negative in the letters and make all your praise very specific.

2. Put the letters in a drawer for a day or two, then take them out and read them. If they still seem inspiring give them to your students.

3. Read one or both letters to the class and ask them to write similar letters to each other. The rules are that everything in the letter must be positive and it must contain specifics.

4. Have students share their letters.

(Note: This can be done weekly in conjunction with a full-class workshop. The writer of the week gets letters of praise from the whole class.)

Questions? Comments? Concerns?

Once we've praised a piece of writing specifically, then the writer will be able to hear our toughest criticism with open ears. It may sound like I'm asking people to flatter each piece of work with some token praise. I'm not. I genuinely believe it is possible to find something good in each piece of writing, and I think you'll find it becomes an acquired skill that is central to being a constructive critic.

One good way to hone our critical skills is to divide our criticism into three categories.

- Questions—these grow out of curiosity about the story or about how the writer wrote it.

- Comments—these can be anything from praise to an idea of a book you think the author would like to read.

- Concerns—these are your toughest criticism and involve problems with the story that need attention, confusing passages, and any suggestions for a new direction.

Dividing criticism into these categories creates a flexibility and balance in the critic's mind. (When I discussed peer conference sheets in the last chapter I expressed these categories with the beginnings of sentences: I like . . . I wonder . . .) If, for example, all my remarks are comments I might ask myself, "Do I have any concerns about this story?" On the other hand, if my remarks are all concerns perhaps I can find something to comment about or ask a few questions. A good way to teach this versatility is for you and your students to use multicolored post-its the way editors do. Questions could be in yellow, comments in green, and concerns in pink.

Another way to teach this skill is to say that all comments and concerns grow out of questions. Ask students to start with questions, then trace them to comments and concerns. This is a more structured approach but it can be very successful with some students.

Here are some general rules I give students for writing on one another's papers.

- Always couch your criticism in the subjective: "This is confusing" becomes "I'm confused here."
- Respond as a reader to things you like right in the place where you read them. Comments like "Wow!" mean a lot to a writer (see earlier section on praise).
- Ask specific questions that flow out of your natural curiosity instead of making suggestions (e.g., instead of "Add more detail" try "What was it like when you walked into the room?").
- Write suggestions in a shared language of craft when possible (e.g., "I want to know more about what she's thinking. Try adding a thoughtshot here.").
- Always write a short note summarizing your feelings about a piece of writing. Begin with something positive. Sign it with your name.

The Red Curse: Grades

In his book *Joining the Literacy Club,* Frank Smith makes a powerful argument for the elimination of grading:

The ultimate response to people opposed to the massive evaluation that infests education today is, "Don't you want children to learn?" No one should get away with a loaded question like that. Proponents of testing and grading should be challenged to demonstrate exactly how they expect evaluation to improve learning and teaching, and to avoid the undesirable consequences. There is no evidence that external control leads to better teachers of better learners. There is a wealth of evidence to the contrary. (1988, 132)

I have a quintessential story about the effect of grades on the writer. She was an older student in one of my night, noncredit, adult classes. The first night she told me how intimidated she was to come, but a friend had convinced her I was a nurturing teacher. She was a fine writer with a fine sensitivity permeating everything she wrote, but she was terrified of being judged. "I had a bad experience in a freshman English class at this school," she said. "I did some of the best writing I've ever done in my life, but at the end the teacher wrote me a really nasty note."

Being curious I asked her who the teacher was. It turned out to be one of the finest in the English department. She told me she still had the note and would bring it to the next class. It went something like this: "Your writing has shown remarkable improvement since the beginning of the semester. You are writing with detail and have a developing sense of voice. You are also beginning to really learn how to organize your thoughts without losing the reader's interest. Great work!!"

This did not strike me as a nasty note. In fact, how could anyone in his or her right mind see this as any more than some good, constructive criticism? However, tucked away in the lower, right-hand corner of the note, just below the signature of this excellent teacher, was a small, barely noticeable letter with a circle around it: C−.

When B. F. Skinner taught at Harvard, he gave A's and incompletes. Everything else, he surmised, was negative reinforcement and would not help his students to learn. There is not one major study that proves that grading helps anyone to learn. There have been hundreds that have proven it is detrimental. Yet educators, administrators, and school board members continue to insist that students be graded, and as long as they do, teachers must devise their own strategies to devalue grades.

Here are some simple suggestions to decrease the negative qualities of grades in your classroom.

- Never grade an individual paper. Rather, grade a student's overall progress as seen in a portfolio, specifying areas of improvement. If you grade a body of work, you will give students a better picture of their overall strengths and weaknesses.

- Discuss the negative qualities of grades with students and be very clear about your desire to have them write for themselves and their audience, not for a grade. (Note: There is an irony here, because only this will get them a higher grade. Reality, unfortunately, isn't always ideal.)

- Create criteria with your students and let them evaluate and grade one another's work in pairs. Ask them to compare their grades for each of the criterion. If they differ by more than one point in their scoring, ask a third student to mediate or do it yourself. The goal here is to find a commonality of language.

- Give students a grade for risk (see chapter 12). Even though this might be a subjective category and differ with each student, without giving it credence there is no way to legitimize its reality. To reward risk with a grade is in some ways the ultimate contradiction because grades encourage the opposite.

For a writing teacher who believes in encouraging revision, graded papers are nothing less than a curse. Low grades discourage and high grades imply that a piece is done. Even worse, students begin writing to improve their grade instead of finding out what they have to say. In reference to the perils of successful publication, Robert Penn Warren said, "Ambition is the death of the poet." Grades, like success, promote ambition, not education. They create and foster a codependent relationship between student and teacher that revolves around the central question "What do you want?" instead of "Why am I here? What can I learn? What do I have to say?" or even, "What can you teach me?" As students wean themselves from external motivators like grades, and as they become empowered to assess their own progress, they begin to understand that learning is much more than receiving praise or enduring punishment; learning is an ongoing personal process that can be both frustrating and fulfilling; learning is its own reward.

The Writer's Struggle

But What If I Can't Freewrite?

Distinct Styles of Revision

There are three rules for writing a novel. Unfortunately,
no one knows what they are.
Somerset Maugham

A teacher at a workshop I gave recently confessed to me guiltily that she had never been able to freewrite properly. "I always cross things out. I can't help it," she said. She had carried this dark secret for years, afraid her peers at the writing-process school where she taught might expose her as an imposter. The only reason she felt safe enough to reveal her secret was because I confessed that I was unable to freewrite in the proper way myself and when I did I rarely produced writing of value to me. Freewriting can be one of the most useful tools for gaining fluency as a writer, but it doesn't help all writers.

The expression of relief on that teacher's face when I said it was OK to cross things out or to stare into space for a while confirmed for me that writing process has gone astray. Teachers have felt increased pressure to teach it as a formula for good writing. They have checklists in the classroom making sure all students web-chart, freewrite, and brainstorm for every story they write, even though these techniques might be totally incongruous with a student's individual writing and revising style. The foolishness of this approach becomes clear when we read interviews with professional writers and interview our own students about their writing habits.

Kurt Vonnegut, Jr., would love to write like William Faulkner, who cranked out *As I Lay Dying* in four weeks, then edited and revised it for another two. But Vonnegut is a self-proclaimed basher who moves sluggishly from sentence to sentence, crumbling up the remains of thoughts that don't move his story ahead. Freewriting is probably something Vonnegut could do, but it probably wouldn't help his writing because that is not the way he thinks.

I teach writing to students in Vermont, and Vermonters are often true to the stereotype of frugal, hardworking people who don't mince words. I often find students who don't like to freewrite because it wastes words. What is remarkable about these students' work is that it often possesses a richer quality of detail than students who are fluent freewriters. I am reminded of an essay by Donald Murray, where he describes his uneasy feeling when faced with a classroom of students that could freewrite at the drop of a hat. He always looked for the students in the back row who stared off into space, thinking. These were often the writers.

Students have different processes of revision, and if we are to teach successfully we must be flexible enough to acknowledge these

unique processes while exposing students to new ideas and techniques. This chapter defines three distinct styles of revision and
shows how to acknowledge them in the classroom with several
exercises. Keep in mind there are several million more.

The Roller Coaster and the Local Train

I don't give a hoot what the writing is like, I write any sort of rub-
bish which will cover the main outlines of the story; then I can
begin to see it.

                                        Frank O'Connor

First I take the roller coaster, then I go back and take the local
train.

                                        Jack McCarthy

This is the most commonly taught style of revision, probably
because it is the most logical and efficient. The writer goes fast on
a first draft, then goes back to revisit. Here's how I teach it.

Taking the Express and Returning on the Scenic Route

1. Tell students, "Today I'm going to teach you one style of revision. It's called The Roller Coaster and the Local Train. First we are going to freewrite like a roller coaster for ten minutes." (Decide on an effective prompt or simply make it an undirected freewrite.)

2. "Now, read over what you wrote and pretend you are taking the local train back through. You can get off wherever you want. Pick a place and add a snapshot, thoughtshot, explode a moment, or just add a detail."

3. "Cross out ten unnecessary words, paragraphs, pages."

Shooting from the Hip

The main rule of a writer is never to pity your manuscript. If you see something is no good, throw it away and begin again. A lot of writers have failed because they have too much pity. They have already worked so much, they cannot just throw it away. But I say that the wastepaper basket is the writer's best friend. My wastepaper basket is on a steady diet.

Isaac Bashevis Singer

The first draft comes from the hand, the second comes from the mind, the last from the heart.

Jon Lassor

This is an important style because it is rarely taught as revision. For students who use this style, revision *is* starting something new, even if the subject seems different. For example, my first story is a ghost story, my second revision is an essay on fear, my third a poem about a haunted house. The writer's struggle to find meaning often transcends genre and even subject. Students need to be taught that revision can mean starting something new. Here's how I try to model it.

Figure 9–1 Web Chart

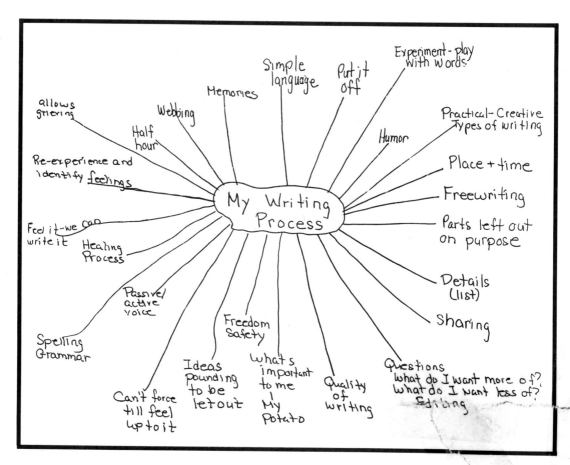

The Shotgun Revisor

1. Students pick a subject rich in meaning (e.g., a person they've known for years, a place they've been to many times). Have them make a web chart about the subject branching off in several directions like the one in Figure 9–1. Ask students to freewrite for ten minutes about one branch.

2. Putting their freewrites aside, students just sit and think about their subject, remembering details and incidents. Have them look back at their web chart for more ideas, then free-write for another ten minutes about a different aspect of their subject. (This step can be repeated.)

3. Students share their pieces. Tell students that one way writers revise is by writing an entirely new thing. Like a person with a shotgun, they blow off revisions in different directions. Each one often gets closer to what they really want to say. (Note: you could also ask students to write in different genres; that is, write a story as a poem and a poem as a story.)

Building the House One Board at a Time

I scratch out a lot, and I never go to the next sentence until the previous one is perfect. Then I type the manuscript and that's it. I never revise.

Cynthia Ozick

I just sit there and stare and wait for the next idea to come.
Dylan Duncan, fourth grade, Chester Andover School

If a sentence doesn't in some way advance the action of the story or reveal character, I cross it out.
Kurt Vonnegut, Jr.

The following exercise is for those students who sit and wait for the idea to come. They write slowly or in quick spurts, waiting for the ideas to crystalize in their minds before putting the pencil to paper. They cross out and add things as they go, not because they are too self-critical but because it helps them to think. They build their stories like houses, one board at a time.

Building A Story

1. "Today we are going to try out a new style of revision. It's especially designed for those who like to write slowly."

2. "We are going to freethink for ten minutes. The rules of freethinking are similar to the rules of freewriting but instead of using a pencil or pen we use our minds. You can think at your desks or go for a short walk. Whatever you do keep thinking about your story. If you are concerned about remembering a good thought, scribble down a line or two."

3. "Stop thinking and start writing. Write for ten minutes. When you get stuck, just stop and think some more."

Danny sat there while the rest of the class scribbled away. He was thinking; he was waiting. I had suggested earlier that he let his mind go wild on the page. After all, this was freewriting time. When I talked with him he explained to me that he was thinking about his story. This was how he always worked. Danny was an eighth grader, and his teacher told me he was the best writer in his class, yet he never brainstormed, he hated web-charting, and he found freewriting impossible. Danny was a writing-process failure, but that didn't stop him from being a wonderful writer.

In an interview Danny told me of his one method of getting unstuck: "I just sit, stare at the wall, and think." Many writers share Danny's method. Indeed many writers, like my ex-teacher, the novelist Thomas Williams, don't distinguish between the time spent sitting and staring and time spent scribbling. "I work for four hours a day," Williams said in an interview. "If I sit there and stare at the page, that's work."

Let your students know that its OK to think.

Oprah and Geraldo Meet the Fifth Grade

The best and most fun way to get your students to think positively and understand their own unique writing styles is to design and produce writer talk shows. For years the *Paris Review* has conducted interviews with professional writers. These interviews have been collected into a series called *Writers at Work,* and they provide great modeling.

When writers talk about their work and their style of writing to a fawning audience they immediately gain authority. Likewise, the interviewer learns to ask questions that reflect and demonstrate his or her own writing process. Talk shows are a wonderful way to acknowledge all the different writing processes in your classroom. They are also a lot of fun.

The TV Talk Show

1. *Modeling.* Talk shows work best after children have published a book. It becomes a way of acknowledging the accomplishment and telling the world. Model the talkshow host in front of the class with a student. Ask questions that expose the revising process, questions like, "What do you do when you get stuck?" or "Does it all come out perfect the first time or do you have to revise?" or "Tell me James, why fish?"

2. *Prepare questions.* Have students read one another's books and prepare questions, some which grow out of the material. I tell kids that the best talk show hosts, like Dick Cavett, really do their homework.

3. *The format.* This can be as complex or as simple as you want to make it. Sometimes I get some instrumental theme music to play as the MC introduces the talk show host. An APPLAUSE card, held up at appropriate moments (commercial breaks and the beginning), is essential. In one residency I did the kids made commercials for reading and writing to go between the interviews. This can be great fun and a way to involve kids who are done with their interviews.

Name that Process—Writing Process Without the Capital P

The more we write and revise, the more we learn about who we are as writers. Asking students to write about their process is one of the best ways to get them thinking about how to solve the problems they face on any writing task. Here are some excerpts from process freewrites that teachers did at a week-long, intensive summer course I taught in Roxbury, Vermont.

Of the three styles mentioned in this chapter, which do you think best describes Lynn Bingham's process?

June 21, 1991 process of writing

Jumping in is what I like to do. No outline, or even conscious thought about what I might do. Somehow—I teach that way—it works well. I have an intuition about where I am going, listen to the tenor of the class—hear the needs of the individual or the

group, smell the next direction. It's what I like about tennis and
golf. The Zen of it, I've heard say. Focus only on the ball. Be the
ball. Never, arm all the way back, follow through, eye on the ball,
level stroke . . . All those things my psyche knows, they are not separate. Nervous. They are my body whole coming to bear on the
ball. Focus on the ball. See it. I like writing like that. My mind a
whole that comes to bear on the page. Smelling when to condense,
when to expand, when to stop and reread. Even the rereading intu-
itively takes in a portion of the whole, magnifies it, strokes it to
feel what is missing, what is crippled, which parts need attention.

Lynn Bingham

Elementary school teacher Nan McBroom describes her process
in more practical terms in her freewrite.

I write best or flow more when it's quiet, when there are no distrac-
tions. I often listen while I write—listen for a reason to look.
Sometimes I get up and walk around, fix a snack, get a drink. It's
my famous procrastination urge. It pulls at me in the back of my
mind saying, "You can't do this. Look! the kitchen's a mess. Maybe
people are hungry. The drain is plugged. Yes, I'll help instead of
writing. No, people are handling it. Doesn't anyone need a
mother?"

Nan McBroom

Louise talks about overcoming the internal obtacles that all
writers face.

My first thought is that I cannot write stories. I can do practical
writing that is required of all of us in our daily lives. This includes
the writing of invitations, notes of appreciation, and formal letters.
In these I am trying to communicate a basic message to someone.

But when someone says, I want you to write about something,
to be creative, I think I can not do it. It is like I panic inside because I know I just can't do this. I found that I would put this off
and find everything else to do and this is not me. I like to get
things done long before they need to be done.

So to begin with I need to forget everything I have been told
about writing and to work through special blocks I associate with
writing. Writing is not about making Art or even trying to make
sense to someone else. Rather it is a way to get around some of my
internal watchers, to get to what it is I need to say.

Louise LaValley

Paulette Darby articulates the connection between her own discovery of her writing self and what she can pass on to her students.

How do I write, let me count the ways, I write from a feeling, an inspiration, a spark that sets off a charge loaded with emotions. I write from anger, fear, passion, belief in a cause or a strong conviction to ideals, or a place in my heart that wells up with tenderness and emotions that spur the desire to savor those feelings. Often, the thoughts come out fragmented and disorganized. I record them on bits and scraps of paper. I recently have learned to use this as an advantage. Shifting the pieces and fitting them into a puzzle in a way that makes the picture complete.

Before I embarked on this journey of "Discovering the Writer Within," I never thought of myself as a writer. I knew I often put pencil to paper to vent my feelings and frustrations. During an extreme period of crisis in my life, about a year ago, I found myself writing ideas and pieces for children's stories. It helped to relax me and direct my attentions away from the craziness around me. I knew I enjoyed reading what I wrote, but I had this choking fear that no one else would value or care about my scribblings. My writings were for me, not for others. I am sure that the fear came from years of school failure as a writer, judged by well-intentioned English teachers who knew how I should write. Even though I was aware of all this it didn't make the risk seem any safer.

Until three weeks ago, when at the age of forty-one, I discovered that the risk is not too great. The experience of our week-long class opened my eyes to my true longing to express and share my writing, and my very soul, with those who choose to listen. I realize I cannot control the reactions of others to my work. I can only control and be true to myself. I feel that I have truly evolved as a writer, and in this continuing evolution I hope to create the space in my classroom for all children to do the same.

Paulette A. Darby

One great way to understand your writing process is to web it. (see Figure 9–1 on page 137.) Try webbing and writing about your own writing process.

Teachers Who Write

All over the country organizations of teachers who write have arisen almost simultaneously with the birth of writing process. This is no surprise. For years researchers like Donald Graves have done work to show that teachers who can model writing process through their own writing have a tremendous advantage in transforming their classroom into a community of writers.

Unfortunately, an obstacle to teachers has been their own educations, which have intimidated, threatened, and red-inked them into submission. In my first book, *Discovering the Writer Within,* I wrote about the Grammar Police, the elite strike force that conducts covert operations in our imaginations, ready to pounce on a dangling participle in a one-hundred-mile radius.

Yes, teachers should write and they *can* write with a little practice and encouragement. And teachers who are ready should also attempt to publish their work. Not only can it be a great supplementary income, but it is a wonderful way to model writing process and seek real editorial advice from students about your story.

Help Me with My Story, Please

1. Try this. Write a book or story appropriate to the grade level you teach. Write a rough draft of your story. Remember, it doesn't have to be perfect. Tell your students where you got your idea and a little about what you were trying to do. You might say something like this: "I've been writing this story but nobody will publish it. Here is my pile of rejections. (I read a few and tell them how it made me feel.) None of them tell me anything about why they don't want it. (Most rejections come in a form letter.) I need your help. As I read this I want you to know what part you like the best, what part the least. I want you to think of questions to help me add detail. I want you to tell me places to add snapshots or thoughtshots.

2. Read your story to the class. Pass out blank paper or the conference forms we talked about in chapter 7. Give them some time on their own to list questions, comments, and concerns.

3. Ask students what questions they have for you.

4. Respond to all the questions that make you think most about the story.

5. Ask students a few questions of your own, such as:

- How can I make the story better?
- Where do you think the big moment in the story is?

6. Thank them for their suggestions and tell them which ones have inspired you, but make sure you let *all* students know their feedback was important to you.

7. Revise your story and revise your revision with the class.

Know Your Watcher

The torch of doubt and chaos, this is what the sage steers by.
Chuang Tsu

Some of you want to skip the last section. "I'm not a writer," you say to yourself. "I don't like writing—never have. That's what bugs me about all this writing process stuff. Just tell me how to teach it and I'll teach it, but why humiliate me?"

If you hate writing and have no desire to write a story, try this exercise.

1. Write a letter to your watcher—the voice inside you that criticizes your ability. It may be a specific teacher or person in your life or it could simply be a part of your personality. You may want to begin by brainstorming a list of influences on your writing or making a timeline of your writing career.

2. Read your letter out loud.

3. Respond to the letter as the child inside you who, like all children, loves to create.

4. Share this dialogue with your students. Explain to them how all writers have a critical side that stops them from writing. Tell them about your teachers. Encourage them to find their own watchers. Ask them to do this exercise.

Recently, a high school teacher told me he felt very insecure about his own writing and didn't feel right about sharing that with his class. He thought it would be bad modeling. I told him I felt just the opposite. When we model our struggles we give our students permission to struggle alongside us. We wipe out the disempowering notion of perfection that teachers often unwittingly model, and we expose our uniqueness, our vulnerability, and most important of all, our humanity.

Spinoffs

- Follow through this exercise by conducting a workshop on stories students feel might be finished. See if they can ask each other questions that give them an idea for a new story or revision.

- If students agree that a piece is ready, encourage them to send it to an appropriate magazine for publication. Have a copy of *Children's Writers and Illustrators Market* in your class-room, which lists names and addresses of hundreds of maga-zines and publishers, and contains information on the publishing process.

- Find ten minutes out of your busy day to write. Donald Graves calls this a "writing occasion." Treat yourself to a pen that you like, a computer, or a notebook. Give yourself per-mission to tell all you have to say.

- After you've written a piece, write yourself a letter of spe-cific praise. Buy yourself a treat. Remember the power of posi-tive reinforcement.

- When you are brave enough, send an essay or story or book to a publisher. If it's accepted for publication, have a party with your class. If you're sent a rejection slip share it with your class. Tell them how it made you feel and explain that all writers, even very famous writers, have had work rejected many times. You might want to make a Rejection Box some-where in the classroom. Each time a student's work is rejected they write their name and the date on the slip and put it in the box. At the end of the year the student with the most rejections wins a Determination Prize.

- Conduct a writing symposium by having your students write down on index cards individual problems they have as writers.

Read the problems one at a time and have the rest of the class make suggestions.

• Write a list of all the teachers you remember in relation to your writing. What did they notice in your writing. What was there that they missed? Write about your best experience writing in school and your worst experience. Share your writing with your class. Have students do the same.

• Make an "unstuck" box, and put it in a convenient location. Ask students to write suggestions for "stuck" writers on index cards and drop them in the box. Encourage students to write down methods that work for them. Stuck writers can use the box as a reservoir of ideas from their fellow writers.

See Dick Revise. Revise, Dick, Revise.

(Revising Basal Readers)

*Who wants to listen to some story about a boy a girl
and a dog trying to climb up a hill and the wagon that
was holding the dog broke or something—It's nothing
to get excited about.*

Josh, fourth grade

I remember Dick and Jane well. They were always running somewhere or other. Actually, that's all I remember. I never learned about Dick's problems tying his shoe or the grief he felt when Spot got hit by a car. I never heard about the night Jane cried when she found out her grandmother would die or the day she spilled cranberry juice on the rug. Perhaps these events were just too difficult to put into simple English. Let me try.

"See Grandmother die."

"Grieve, Jane, grieve."

"Die, Grandmother, die."

Basal readers have helped millions of children to gain confidence in their reading, but they also have taught those same children that reading could be somewhat, if not totally, boring. My daughter Jessie's class still uses basal readers. Sometimes I go in and watch the children read. They do it in pairs. I think it's in order to keep each other awake in case they nod off in mid-sentence. My daughter has her own books and loves to read. In some ways basal readers have helped her to know the difference between literature and drivel, but on another level it has just deadened her interest and her confidence that words can relay meaning.

Recently I have been an artist-in-residence at a school that is switching over from basals to a whole-language, literature-based program. There are still many of the old readers lying around and I picked up one and started reading about a sad man running to Nan who had a fan.

Heady stuff. There was a picture of a man sweating and a kangaroo fanning herself, the text made up of meaningless, monosyllabic rhymes. I was about to walk into a sixth-grade class. The day before, the kids had written questions to each other between the lines of their stories, but they didn't know what to do with them. Their teacher had restructured their entire curriculum from the traditional drill-and-kill worksheet to a dynamic collaborative learning environment.

"They were taught to be passive learners," she told me the day before. "Give them a stack of worksheets, and they'll sit there all day doing them." It was no wonder that they had some difficulty asking questions and answering them in their own work. But today I had just thought of a wonderful way to make use of all these puerile readers I had been tortured with since I was six years old. I would teach the sixth graders to revise basal readers. (See Figure 10–1.)

Figure 10–1   Questions and Answers

Why Did The sad man fun?
Who was Nan?
Why did the story ryhme?
Why did he run to Nan?
Why did Nan fan the sad Man?
Why did the author write this
       story?

Why did he run?
Because some one made fun of him.
Why was he sad?
Big Bully Bruno was teasing him?
Why did he run to Nan?
Because Nan was his grandmother and
                she will protect him.
What was the sad man's name?
  Brendon.
Why did Nan fan the sad man?
To Dry his tears.
Whe does Brendon live?
Bel Air
Grandma's name is NAN NAN.
Where did Nan get the fan?
Cheap yardsale is fro across from
            Osco in Globe plaza
            in Stratham Moo
                     Hampshire

   Moral - Never buy cheap fan
in Stratham Moo Hampshire

Revising a Basal

1. Photocopy a section of an old basal reader at the top of a blank piece of paper. Leave plenty of space beneath. Talk to students about basal readers. Ask their opinions. Ask students if they know what the expression "reading between the lines" means. Tell them you are going to teach them to write between the lines, to tell the rest of the story.

2. Ask students to pair up or break into small groups, no more than four to a group. (Because this is sort of a silly activity, I think kids do it better and have more fun in groups.) Read the piece aloud and ask students to write questions between the lines. Make it clear that the best questions will help to add more information to the story.

3. Students write ten to fifteen details about the characters and story, using their questions as a guide.

4. Students rewrite the story on a separate piece of paper.

5. Students share the stories with the whole class and talk about how questions help writers to see more and more.

The sixth graders at Halifax School loved this exercise. They did it in pairs, and ten minutes into the writing they were already asking, "Can I be first to share?" As they read back their steamy romances, horror stories, and funny nonsense stories, I couldn't help feeling they were somehow taking revenge for the hours they were forced to spend reading these dumb, condescending books.

Listen to what the fourth-grade critics in Deborah Craig's class at Stratham Memorial School say when you ask them about basals. It's almost as if they're telling war stories—wars against boredom.

BL:	Do you like reading them?
Mike:	No.
BL:	Why?
Mike:	Because they're boring.
BL:	Why are they boring?
Mike:	Because it like says, "The dog crossed the road and then he went to his house." They're just little sentences.

Billy: There's no description.
           I don't like basals because the whole class has to
           read them, and like someone will tell you what's going
           to happen on the way to school and it won't be a sur-
           prise. I also think they're boring, because all it says is
           "Spot ran to get the ball."
BL: Why don't you care about Spot?
Billy: Because he's a dog.
Kelly: In second grade we all had these groups and we had
           these basal books and we each read from different
           groups, and they were really boring because when
           you'd read it it would be just something really simple
           and they wouldn't have any depth or dialogue or good
           description or anything. I mean, the closest you'd get
           to description was like, "Spot was a dog" or some-
           thing. It doesn't give you a picture of it. They'd show
           these two people walking down the street, and in the
           story it says they're walking down the street to school.
           . . . I'm sure when they write them, they don't really
           put a lot of thought into them.
Jenny: They're all informational in a way that tells just what
           they did. Now I read series and mysteries and biogra-
           phies and stuff like that.
BL: But aren't basals easier to read?
Jenny: Yes, and they're easier to understand, but when a class
           reads a whole bunch of different books you learn about
           different things.
BL: Why do you think they make them in the first place?
Jenny: Because they were really simple books that no one had
           to put a lot of thought into and they teach kids how
           to read, but they don't get into detail about anything
           and they show you the setup of a story.
BL: How do they compare to literature?
Scott: They're really boring now because they were like,
           "The man is funny," like stuff like that and now when
           you read a book it's got a lot of detail in it. The bas-
           als, they didn't have a lot of detail in them. The thing
           about basals is they don't really tell a lot of informa-
           tion. Instead of saying, "The boy jumped up from his
           seat and ran outside," it'll say, "The boy went outside.
           The boy played ball." It doesn't give any detail about
           how he did it.

Lindsay: Some of the stories have no meaning, like one time we read about how leaves grow and how this little boy thought that leaves were a bear. I mean it was so, so stupid.

Scott: I think they're boring because it would just tell stories like, "Jane ran to Spot and Spot ran to Jane" or something like that.

Josh: It doesn't have any meaning to it. It's just some short story. There's no character in it. It doesn't give any information. You sit there and read these boring, boring stories.

   In my old school we did have plays and stuff like that from the basals but they didn't have no meaning. I mean, who wants to listen to some story about a boy, a girl, and a dog trying to climb up a hill and the wagon that was holding the dog broke or something? It's nothing to get excited about. Take a book like this with a title like, "Fourth Graders Don't Believe in Witches." It has a meaning.

What strikes me about these fourth graders' view of basal readers is that it is so much like any rational adult's view might be. Though today's basals often contain "real" literature the issue of choice still remains. The students at Stratham Memorial School have been lucky enough to choose their own books from many different genres and develop a critical sensibility. Think about the millions of children who have only read basal readers and been given dull workbooks to fill out. These children will tell you straight out that reading and writing are boring. They have been denied a chance to love reading and writing in the name of functional literacy. Tell me that this makes sense.

The same denial exists in classrooms where teachers refuse to allow children to write and choose their own subjects until they have mastered grammar. In Vermont, there is an attitude toward education that turns up almost every March at town meeting time. It goes something like this: We spend so much money on our schools and our kids can't even spell. I think we were better off back in the days of the one-room schoolhouse when we didn't have all these fancy ideas like meaning!

I sometimes see it in the eyes of parents when I explain process writing at P.T.O. meetings. Sometimes, a parent will ask me point blank if process writing and whole language are really necessary.

I'm never quite sure what to say. Sometimes I carefully and patiently explain that a holistic curriculum encourages children to be thinkers as well as learners. I try to talk about the importance of choice and responsibility in the world we live in. I criticize traditional, passive learner instruction, which teaches students to search for the right answer instead of the ability to explore solutions. I make brilliant appeals to reason, eloquent pleas, but when students like Jen Lucca in Deborah Craig's fourth-grade class at Stratham Memorial School speak up about why they want to read and think, the message is stronger than anything I could hope to say. Keep the following letter handy and pass it on to those few parents who don't seem to understand your efforts to empower students.

Let Kids Choose What They Want To Read

Jennifer Lucca

The way you read pretty much depends on where you read. For instance, the way I read now, at SMS is different than the way I used to read at my old school, SHS. Why? Well, because at SMS we read "independently" and at SHS we read out of basals. (Reading "independently" means you read what you want to read and not out of a basal.) At SMS we have a choice of what we read. We can read pretty much ANYTHING we want. We can read mysteries, biographies, fiction, and everything else.

Sometimes our teacher will have us read a certain genre of reading. For instance, say our teacher assigned us to read a historical fiction story. She tells us what *type* of book, not *what* book. So she lets us have a choice of what books we do and don't read.

I like the way we read for several reasons. 1) Because we have a lot of CHOICES. (That's what I've been trying to tell you.) 2) Because we have choices *we* get to pick what we want to read. We know what we like to read, so when we get to pick we'll pick what we like to read, and we'll be HAPPY! If kids/adults like what they read then they're more apt to read more. (You see, I think that if kids/adults like what they read they will be encouraged to read more.) 3) Because I like being able to read stuff that interests me and stuff that I like, not stuff that bores me and stuff I don't like.

When you read "independently" you get to read books that you could never read in a basal. Like now I read series and occasionally I read a choose-your-own-adventure book. If I still read out of a basal there is no way I could read them. Some other books that you can't read if you read in a basal are: mysteries, choose-your-own-adventure, comics/cartoons, humor, biography/autobiography, fiction, series, adventure, awards, fairy tale/myth, fantasy, historical fiction, poetry/drama, science fiction . . . I could go on forever naming them all but I won't. The only things you can read about in a basal are informational things like: "How to plant a tree" or "Jim and Bill make cookies using a measuring cup." They are usually about the same characters: Jane, Bill, Jim, Hosa, Kim, and a dog named Spot. They are pretty boring characters because they don't change and they basically have no personality. For instance, I'm reading *The Great Gilly Hopkins* by Katherine Paterson. I really liked the story for 2 reasons. 1) I like Gilly, the main character, because of her personality. She's a foster child and from her experiences she became tough and has a personality that says "Nobody's going to push me around." Not in a million years would there be a character like that in a basal. All the characters in a basal are nearly perfect. They're polite, nice, well-behaved, and well, PERFECT! That sort of reminds me of TV. Like the characters on "The Cosby Show" are nearly perfect and the characters on "The Simpsons" are characters we can relate to a little better. I think that people like books better if they can relate to them. When I read out of a basal I hated to read because the only thing I read was a basal and the stories in it didn't interest me, so I didn't like reading in general. Once I came to SMS and started reading books and not basals, I realized reading was fun. The more I read, the more I enjoyed reading. Soon I was reading so much my mother had to tell me to put my book away and go outside to get some fresh air. Then I would take my book outside and I would read there. I love to read that much!

Back to basals. Say I was really into reading about birds and my friend really liked to read mysteries. If we read out of a basal and the story was about birds, I would probably enjoy the story and my friend wouldn't. If we read on our own we'd each choose a story we liked and we'd *both* be happy instead of just *one* of us being happy.

If you ask me I think reading a book is a lot more fun than reading a basal. If I had the choice of reading either a basal or a book I would choose a book any day!

Spinoffs

- Have students write questions between the lines of a partner's story, Ask students to circle any questions that make them want to write more, and then freewrite for ten minutes.

- If they're not already, have your students keep a reading journal. Let them choose their own books to read and write letters to you about them. (See chapter 7.)

- Read with your class during silent reading time. Share with them what you're reading and what your writing. (See chapter 7.)

- Point out elements of craft to students when you come across good examples in your reading. Model reading as a writer, and when you read them your own writing refer to elements of craft when appropriate.

- Evaluate a piece of basal writing with your students, then evaluate a piece of real literature and compare evaluations. This is a wonderful way to get students beyond general comments, like "It's boring," to more specific criticism.

- Have students write an extra chapter to a published book they didn't want to have end.

- Ask students to revise the first few pages of a book they felt was too slow-moving. Ask them to begin by circling a new lead later in the chapter.

- Have students keep lists of their favorite books. Ask them to write thumbnail descriptions of what makes them so good on index cards. These cards can be kept on file or in pockets on the back covers of the books. Potential readers can get a quick glimpse of what their classmates have to say.

eleven

Voice and Choice:

Nurturing Voice and Tone in Student Writing

The mind working alone produces thought; the heart produces feeling; the tongue makes speech and the hand in isolation makes scribble: all four together create voice.

Geof Hewitt

I had chosen the voice committee because that's my overall favorite quality in a piece of writing. That's what I look for as a reader and teacher. That's what makes me smile—seeing a kid's voice leap off the page, speaking to you directly like some hotline to the soul. It was also a quality in writing that was hard to break down and teach. If it was there, great. There's a writer. But if it wasn't could you say to a child "I want you to put some voice into this"? Voice was a mystery, or a condition as much as a quality in the writing.

I was on the benchmark team for Vermont's statewide portfolio assessment. My job, along with two other teachers, was to find examples of voice in all four categories of proficiency to serve as benchmarks for the training of assesors. Myself and nine other teachers had holed up at the Coolidge Hotel in White River Junction, Vermont, with over five hundred student portfolios.

The Coolidge, named after Vermont's favorite son Calvin Coolidge, was a late nineteenth-century wonder that had fallen into decay and elegant funkyness in the latter twentieth century. There were a few permanent residents, housed by the state as part of their deinstitutionalization from mental health facilities. Some of the other rooms were let out to Dartmouth College students, and on weekends they ran $200.00-a-head murder mysteries, prom nights, and just about anything else they could think of to bring in some extra cash. The Coolidge had a voice all its own, from the Buddy Rich drum solos the plumbing played deep into the night to the 3 A.M. whistle of the northbound freight train to Quebec to the campy jokes of the waiters who took refuge in the third-floor rooms.

Geof Hewitt, Vermont's writing consultant to secondary schools, had chosen the Coolidge despite concerns that a more appropriate place, like the Holiday Inn conference center, would be a safer bet. But now as we sat in the Coolidge, pawing through the boxes of student portfolios under a portrait of Calvin looking on with mock determination with a cat wailing in the alley, it seemed impossible to imagine doing this anywhere else. It was the unique character of this hotel that underscored our search for unique voices in student's writing.

The ten teachers sat in clusters in the dark lobby of the upstairs. For the most part they were absorbed in student writing, but every once in a while someone would laugh and share a tidbit of detail or an interesting teacher assignment. In the afternoon we reconvened as a large group and found that many of the same student papers had jumped out at us from the stacks of boxes. We had come expecting to be chained to a desk, pouring over illegible student handwriting like well-meaning, burned-out teachers. Nobody expected it to be a joyous celebration of student writing. Nobody thought it would be so much fun.

It was sometimes easier to find voice in the writing of fourth graders than it was in the eighth-grade work. This seemed to contradict a frequently debated assertion that a particular work deserved a higher rating because it was developmentally the best that a fourth or eighth grader could do. If voice was developmental, it was hard to understand why fourth graders sometimes had it but eighth graders didn't.

This was not a surprise to me after having taught freshman English in college for years. I've come to call it the Invasion of the Voice Snatchers. Students often begin my course with little or no voice in their writing. For years they have conformed their writing to teachers' assignments, patterned their words and ideas around easy academic formulas, such as the five-paragraph theme, research paper, book report, etc. They've learned to write answers instead of questions (see chapter 1). They have not written anything to discover for themselves what they *might* know but have written to convince teachers of what they *do* know.

Finding a voice is a slow process that begins with teaching students to value their own experiences and perceptions and to write them down. Students with the strongest voices often have kept journals for years. They've learned to translate their thoughts into words without letting their audience block them out. They sense the importance of what they are saying and struggle to say it better.

Voice is not something that can be taught in a step-by-step fashion. Imagine the absurdity of a baby being taught to speak by her parents and you have a pretty good idea of the absurdity of teaching voice. However, given the wrong environment a child may never learn to speak. We've all read stories of feral children raised by wolves or locked in bedrooms for their formative years who are unable to learn language. Teachers, like good parents, can create an environment in the classroom that encourages their students to write with individual voices. And they can also define voice for their students. Here are a few basic ideas for promoting and teaching a sense of voice in the classroom.

Nurturing Voices

1. Get students writing on topics of their own choice regularly. Voice seems to develop out of practice and having something to say.

2. Ask students to imitate a voice of a distinctive character from a book or a distinctive character from their lives. Or have them try finding a voice for an electric can opener, for example. (Imitation is often a playful way of finding voice, like putting on masks.)

3. Incorporate letter writing into the day. Whether it's writing letters to peers or letters to you about their response to a movie, play, or book, students need to understand that they have opinions and that those opinions matter. The kids with the loudest voices are often those with the most to say.

4. Teach students to write fast and often, letting their thoughts leak through.

5. Show students how to get personality into even the most rigid forms of writing, like resumes and assigned essays. Save examples of student papers that break the mold.

6. Encourage students to make their awkwardness work for them. If they can't describe the beauty of a sunset, they can write about how they can't describe the beauty of a sunset. If they are honest then their voice will emerge. Remember voice is questions, not answers.

Writers who write with voice or expressive tone constantly make choices that reflect a personal interest in their subject. Writers who lose their voice are often blindly following an outline or laundry-list form (e.g., the five-paragraph theme, the research report, the biography). Here is a quick lesson to get students understanding the connection between voice and choice.

Voice and Choice

I begin a lesson on voice and choice by reading the first few paragraphs of Russell Freedman's biography of Abraham Lincoln.

Freedman begins with an eloquent, well-rendered description of Lincoln's physique, then moves to a funny story of how Lincoln used his homeliness to his advantage during debates. Next I read the encyclopedia's entry on Lincoln. I ask students to notice the details that Freedman chooses to include and compare them to the arbitrary list-like description in the encyclopedia. We talk about how writers who are following their own interest in a subject constantly choose which details to include when, while writers who are trapped by a form seem to have no say in the matter. I explain how even intimidating forms like job resumes and research papers should contain a personal expression of the author.

Sometimes I give examples, like the teacher I know who asked her second grade to help her write her job resume for the Curriculum Director's position she had applied for. They made it like a children's picture book, with photographs of all the things she'd done in the classroom. Needless to say, it stood out from all the other boring resumes, which sounded professional with all the right buzz words but contained nothing to make them stand out. She got the job.

How many biography papers have you read that begin, "_____ was born in 1853"? Writers who know about choice can start a biography anywhere. Here's how to teach it.

1. Students pair up and interview each other for five minutes each about their lives. Explain to them that as biographers they are digging for interesting facts about the person. Start by brainstorming a list of questions.

2. After both students have collected facts, have them circle the most telling detail and turn it into a lead.

3. Students share leads and talk about how boring the biographies would be if they began, "_____ was born in 1984."

4. Discuss how powerful writers follow their own curiosity, not a prescribed form.

When I used to teach the research paper to college freshmen I'd begin by telling my students that there were thousands of ways to write an interesting research paper and only one way to write a boring one. Unfortunately, that was the way many of us learned. That's because we were taught how to write a research paper instead of why we should bother. As students learn to find their excitement in the facts they uncover, they immediately begin breaking the mold and making choices. Of course, a personal voice might not be appropriate for a report on the mating habits of a wasp, but if it's an interesting paper, the curiosity of that author will be present on every page in the choices that author has made. An effective tone is a strong voice in disguise. In the next two sections of this chapter, I'll show you ways to teach tone to your students.

Audience and Voice

Kathy assured me that she wasn't a writer. She was a waitress in a restaurant where I cooked several winters ago, and one night after work I had engaged her in a conversation about writing. She told me about all the strict grammarian teachers she had throughout her life, especially in parochial school, where one eraser mark was tantamount to a class felony. "I know how to write, don't get me wrong," she said. "I'm just not a writer."

"What exactly do you mean by that?" I asked.

"I mean, I'm not good at writing formal papers. I'm great at grammar but I just don't like it."

We talked for a while longer. Kathy was a young woman with strong opinions and able to articulate them well. I found myself getting angry at all those teachers with all their little assignments who had successfully convinced her that she was not a writer. Then, almost as an aside to assuage my anger she said, "I *do* love writing letters though. My friends save all my letters. They say it's just like I am there talking with them."

Kathy's story reminds us that audience is the key to finding a voice. When kids start writing to their friends instead of some distant, form-conscious teacher, their voices naturally develop. When teachers give up their role as corrector and become genuine readers, students begin responding in their own voices and not some stilted cross between expectation and assignment. Throughout this book I have thrown out ideas for teaching revision, but the keystone for revision is the writer's sense of a captive audience and what he or she wants to say to that audience.

The other element at work is the writer's perception of audience and how it affects a piece of writing. This can be called *tone* and, as in speech, it is a reflection of how a person modulates his or her voice. David, a blonde-haired, soft-spoken sixth grader at Randolph Village School, succinctly explained to me what tone is. He said, "It's like kids' voices. They have their playground voices and they have their classroom voices. You have to know when to use each one."

Here are several exercises to make students aware of the importance of tone in their writing.

Whom Are You Writing To? Teaching Tone

1. Have students write a letter of apology to a neighbor for a window they accidentally broke. Tell them to be polite and soft-spoken. When they are done, have them then write a letter of apology to their brother or sister for something they did that they're not sorry for. This time tell them to be rude and obnoxious. Share the letters and discuss the different tones.

2. Find a boring piece of writing, an insurance policy or a memorandum, perhaps from the Central Office somewhere. Give a portion of it to your students and have them rewrite it so a five-year-old could understand it. Share the rewrites. Note the qualities of each tone.

3. Write a boring job résumé or use one you've already written if it has phrases like, "implemented curricula in an integrated holistic manner." Explain to students that the reason you wrote it this way was because you thought it would impress administrators. Now tell them you've decided to forget about that audience and write it to your best friend. Photocopy portions or use overheads to demonstrate how sometimes shifting your concept of audience helps you to achieve a clearer tone.

4. Ask students to imagine a character who is staying at camp for the first time. Have them write two letters, one to his/her worried parents and one to his/her best friend. Have them describe what they did on a day when they got in trouble with the camp counselor.

We have a word in speech to describe a speaker who talks with powerful personal expression combined with an appropriate tone for the occasion. We say they're eloquent. As students gain a concept of their own voices as writers, they learn to adapt them to different purposes and forms without losing their unique personality. They learn eloquence in writing. When we nurture and praise voice in our students' writing we imply that writing is much more than the basic ability to communicate in various social forms effectively; it is a way of expressing who we are. Teaching voice begins with acknowledging and valuing the uniqueness of every student in your classroom.

Toby Treu teaches fourth grade in Chester-Andover School in Chester, Vermont. Like many of the best writing teachers I've seen, her desk is buried in books and papers and her class functions like a community of writers and thinkers. She is not the police force, or the judge, but more like the head of a large family who administers justice and compassion alternately throughout the day. But the thing that impresses me most about Ms. Treu is the expression on her face when one of her fourth graders hands her a story. She could have seen it a hundred times, it could be scrawled in smudged pen or smeared with erasure marks, but when a child hands her a story to read, her face beams with delight.

Like infants who coo at their adoring parents, voices grow when teachers delight in student writing.

Spinoffs

- Read a boring, voiceless research paper or encyclopedia entry to the class. Brainstorm ways to make it more interesting and then ask students to find their own encyclopedia entry at the library, which they can rewrite, letting their own interest choose what facts go first. Share revised entries and talk about the connection between voice and choice.
- Read out loud portions of a book with a strong voice in it—books like *Catcher in the Rye* or *Winnie the Pooh.* Discuss the qualities and how the voice reveals them.
- Re-tell a fairy tale from a different point of view in the first person. ("My name is Goldilocks and I got a story to tell you about the weirdest restaurant I've ever been to. It's called the

Bears Three and I wouldn't recommend it.") Point out to students how shifting point of view helps them to escape the old storyteller voice that they may be bored with.

- Give students an intimidating writing assignment, like a college entrance essay. Have them freewrite it as if they were writing to their best friend.

- Have students pretend they are a wealthy upper-crust person like Prince Perfect or the Dutchess of Decorum. They're to freewrite about a dreadful incident that happened recently, such as stepping in dog poo. Then students pretend they are a person of the working classes—a cab driver, a farmer, a waitperson—and they describe seeing Prince Perfect or Dutchess Decorum stepping in the dog poo. Students share pieces and note how some people use language to disguise reality and others embrace it. They and you will probably also laugh a lot, taking joy in how language and voice enrich our experiences.

- Have students keep a journal and write daily. Voice comes with fluency of thought to page.

When writer Andy Green does an in-service workshop on voice, he quotes what Louie Armstrong said about jazz: "I don't know how to define it, but I know it when I hear it." The best way to make your students aware of voice is to read them pieces and teach them to listen for it. Find examples of your students' work like this piece written by Sara Katz, an eighth grader from Cabot, Vermont.

A First Experience

by Sara Katz (8th grade)

It was a weekend day that was cast over with a layer of clouds. Every once in awhile the meek sun peeked out and then quickly disappeared.

"We've gotta load the truck today, guys," Dad announced.

Of course we groaned because he was talking about wood. None of us like to stack wood. "You want to stay warm this winter, don't you?" Of course I do, and even I, the Queen of Smart Mouth can't think of a quick and witty retort that would prove him wrong in some way.

Today was a different sort of day, though. I was feeling particularly energetic and happy. For the most part I was cooperative about getting ready to go out. I felt like a real wood woman when I was finished dressing for the wood pile-my size 9 winter Thinsulate boots, a big burly jacket, mittens three sizes too big and to top the out fit off, I wore my hair in a ponytail on the top of my head. A true wood woman.

(You know, it can get very embarassing when you're standing in your yard looking like a real idiot, throwing wood onto a 1963 Ford truck, and people you know start driving by.)

Dad usually splits the wood and then throws it into a pile. Well, there's usually more than one pile and they're all lined up. So when you finish one pile you back the truck up to the next pile. And on this certain day, Dad announced that I was going to learn to do something I'd wanted to do for years: drive the truck.

"Okay. Make sure it's in neutral. It's the one in the middle that wiggles. Yeah, that's it. Now, turn the key and press the gas pedal."

I did exactly what he said, but the engine roared.

"Not so far! Take your foot off the gas pedal."

I did that but the engine still roared.

"Pull it out with your foot." I looked at him in confusion. "It's stuck." I sighed and reached down to pull the gas pedal back. I'd forgotten that this was a 1963 green Ford dump truck we were talking about here. It didn't even have seatbelts.

"Okay, just practice pressing the clutch and letting it out slowly. Good. Now put it in reverse."

"Where's reverse?"

He told me but the truck began to go forward when I let go of the clutch. I panicked and began pressing on all the pedals at once hoping I'd hit the brake. It stalled.

"Get out, you flunked."

Oops.

Dad let me try driving a second time, but I still couldn't find reverse.

We were almost finished and Dad let me try again, my last chance to prove I could do it. The truck was in an eerie position: behind a tree. That meant I'd actually have to steer!

I turned the key, put her in first and I couldn't believe it but I actually drove! I got past the tree but my victory didn't last long. All of the sudden I started bumping all around. It was very confusing. I could barely make out what they were saying outside the truck.

"What are you doing?" Dad was shouting.

"Turn, turn!" Jon cried.

The truck was stuck in something and wouldn't go, forward, so I stopped pressing the gas.

Dad was yelling when I looked out the window and I noticed that I was stuck in a pile of wood. I felt sure I'd ruined the truck and Dad was going to kill me. To my surprise, he laughed.

"I think you better wait awhile. You really need some pork to drive this thing."

A first experience. You can actually have fun on a gloomy November day stacking wood.

twelve

I Probably Shouldn't Hand This to an English Teacher

Risk and Writing

We are, each one of us, our own prisoner. We are locked up in our own story.
Maxine Kumin

There are always a few in every school I visit. Sometimes they are girls but more often they are boys. They tend to hunker around the edges of the classroom like little James Deans and Jodie Fosters. And if they write anything at all on their paper, it is often copied from a neighbor or something they saw on TV. Ask them to revise and they look at you and tell you two words: "It's done." These are the students who write THE END in big letters, filling the rest of the page. It is almost as if they are afraid of all the stuff inside them that could sneak out if they let their guard down.

Some teachers give them their own little areas in the back of the classroom; more progressive teachers mix them in. But the fact remains—these are the scared, troubled children who hold their imaginations at gunpoint. How can we teach them to write? How can we teach them to revise?

Two students come to mind: one twenty-two-year-old man from my classes in Vermont prisons, one fourth grader from a classroom in Vermont. Rick, the prisoner, would not write a word for the first five classes. He would joke with the other prisoners and try to distract them from their writing. He would steal milk from the milk machine in the cafeteria where I held class. I suppose if he were in school he would have been labeled a troublemaker, but in jail such a distinction has little meaning. Furthermore, my classes were voluntary, so it wasn't as if he were being held there against his will. What was even more puzzling was that one by one all the other students in the class started writing, and soon there was no one to make trouble with. He finally was reduced to just sitting there chewing on his pencil, but he still wouldn't write.

I had done everything in my power to teach him that writing was real, not something you learned in school. I had the students write about their fathers, mothers, friends, places they knew, fantasy islands. I taught them how to make things real by using detail and chronicling their passion for a subject. I felt like a prize fighter throwing all my best punches and watching my opponent just sit there, unimpressed. Then one day something happened.

It was a simple, deceptively simple, assignment. Write a bad poem about a moment in time. The poem had to be bad if they were to do the assignment correctly. This was, I think, the thing that inspired Rick to write "Snake Stew":

Snake Stew

Hey mom I brought you something to put in the stew your making.

You should have seen the look on her face when I handed her
the garter snake I had peeled off the road.

I can still remember her words exactly.

You get that snake out of here right now or I'm gonna kick
your ass.

Funny thing, but when he read his piece to the class Rick
turned beet red with embarrassment. The class loved it and I told
him he had failed to do the assignment. I had asked for a bad poem
not a good poem. He insisted that it was a bad poem. He said he
thought it was dumb and he couldn't understand why I liked it so
much. However, something fundamental had changed in his attitude toward writing.

I saw him after class scribbling a few lines in his journal. The
next class he showed me a serious poem he had written. It was
about his quest for understanding the patterns of betrayal in his
life. It was a prayer to God. It was not half as good as "Snake Stew"
in my opinion, but that didn't really matter. To Rick this was real
writing and he had written it. In some basic way it was his revision
of "Snake Stew," Rick's way of pulling away from what happened
in his painful childhood and crying out for forgiveness.

Suddenly Rick, who had dropped out of high school, was writing
regularly. He still liked to steal milk from the milk machine. He
still enjoyed disturbing his classmates, but despite all previous odds
he had now joined them. He was scribbling with his Bic pen in
his composition book.

Students like Rick often make assumptions about what writing
is. A teacher can tell them how to loosen up, a teacher can model
the power of true writing a million times, but until that student
makes a discovery through his or her own writing, all other efforts
are almost pointless. I once told a teacher I felt the most important
thing writing teachers can do is give their students pencils and
paper and tell them to write. Rick needed a little more than that.
He needed that fundamental understanding that writing is real,
writing matters.

Luc was a fourth grader who sat in the back row, an aide perched
at his side. He hated writing, and revising was just more of the
same in his mind. The kids around him were writing pages about
aliens from outer space, Captain Skyhawk superheroes, monsters
with missions. He sat there with a numb look on his face. He
created disturbances whenever possible, wrinkling his lined paper
and heaving it at the girl in the front row who was writing about

an imaginary friend. The teacher had already confided in me that Luc had an IEP and not to expect very much.

"I want you to write about a place," I said to him.

"A made-up place?"

"No, a real place, a place you have been."

"That's easy," he said, picking up his chewed pencil with a sort of mock piousness. He was a skinny blonde-haired child, and when he smiled at me he seemed to gloat. I came back a few minutes later and he had written one short sentence: "I went to Maine." The rest of the page was filled with THE END in nine-inch letters.

I conferenced with Luc.

"That's an interesting story," I said. "Can you tell me more?"

"No, it's done." He smiled at me, a sort of smug smile. He had impenetrable brown eyes. He made me feel like some venerable gentleman who could comment at length about the disrespect children show their elders. He made me feel old.

"What happened when you went to Maine?" I asked.

"I saw my father," he said.

I handed him a new piece of paper. "Write about that."

I walked away before he could reply. This is my harried teacher technique. I pretend like I'm rushing off to see another student, but really I am trying to avoid Luc's attempt to deflect my suggestion.

A few minutes later I felt a tugging at my sleeve. It was Luc. "I want to show you my story."

I followed him back to his desk. He had written half a page this time before writing THE END, and the letters of THE END were noticeably smaller. Without even reading a word I could tell we were making progress. He insisted on reading it to me, another good sign. He read slowly, pausing after each word.

"I went to maine. I saw my father there. I hadn't saw him in three years. We had fun. THE END"

I praised him and told him his story was very powerful, that kids with separated parents would really relate to it. Then I asked him, "What did you do in Maine?" He started to tell me, and I told him to write it down.

Luc eventually wrote a one-page story about his trip to Maine. He made it into a book and read it to the class. Like Rick, Luc needed to discover that writing was not something a teacher told him to do, but something real and as much a part of him as anything he had ever said or done.

I occasionally teach freshman English at the college level. At least once a semester a student will come up to me with his or her best paper to date and hesitantly say, "I probably shouldn't hand this to an English teacher." Usually, this paper reveals personal feelings, experiments with a bizarre voice, or displays a high concentration of imaginative fervor, like a paper I once got called, "The Day in the Life of a Gummy Bear." When students step outside the assumptions of who they are and what they should be writing, they take a risk and feel they need to warn you. Like Luc writing about his long lost father, or Rick facing his past and praying for a new life, they have put aside their deadening expectations of what school should be and begun writing for personal satisfaction. They are learning to be surprised by their words; they are learning that writing is fun.

Maybe you have a student like Ric or Luc sitting in your classroom. During writing time she writes a sentence or two and then crosses it out. Last year's teacher has already informed you she is not a writer but you haven't given up yet. You are looking for a way to light a fire in her pen but she struggles to do the bare minimum and tells you straight out, "I hate writing."

How do you encourage students to overcome their limits, to take the necessary leap into their writing? How do you teach risk?

Teaching Risk

1. Define and model risk for your students. It can be as simple as, "Risk is when you do something you have never done before." Tell them about the first time you jumped out of an airplane or got married. Ask them to describe a time they took a risk and did something new. It doesn't have to be a big thing. Ask them to freewrite about it for ten minutes.

2. Talk about how writers are always taking risks, trying new things, experimenting with new genres and voices. "Today each of us is going to take a risk. Make a list of possible things that could be risky for you to write. It could be something personal, it could be a new form for you, like poetry or mystery stories. It could just be writing in a different voice or in the third person. Make a list of a few risky areas. Pick one and write."

3. Students share their work in small groups or a large group, depending on the level of trust in the class. Have them talk about why their writing was risky and what it was like to try something new.

The first step in encouraging risk is to create a safe environment for experimentation in the classroom. Teachers who simply tell their students to write about anything will find a status quo quickly develop in the classroom. Whether it's boys who all write skateboarding or sports stories or girls who fantasize about romance or careers, it's important to make note of the current genres and model alternatives to both the stuck writers like Rick and those who have let themselves get into ruts.

Risk taking is often accompanied by queasiness and unsure feelings. If a teacher can provide encouragement or praise for a student's new direction it may be all that student needs to keep going. The preceding exercise is meant to begin this process. Professional writers often seek out readers, such as agents or editors, who will simply give them a pat on the back as they embark on a new project. Young writers need the same.

For Luc, taking a risk was simply writing about something real that was important to him. A year from now it might be making up a superhero and dressing him in a purple raincoat with yellow boots, as opposed to the way his neighbor Patrick dresses Captain Skyhawk. For Rick, it was encountering his childhood and touching upon the deep reservoir of sadness and despair inside him. A week from now it may be creating an imaginary prisoner who escapes and moves through the woods to the Canadian border. There is no intrinsic standard of risk. It varies from writer to writer, from piece to piece. It is the teacher's job to recognize it and praise it so that student can move ahead with his or her writing and go where no writer has ever gone before.

Spinoffs

- Pick five students in your class. Examine their writing and decide what types of subjects or approaches might be risky for them. Try giving them suggestions in those areas. Remember that for some writers personal nonfiction subjects are risky, for others it may be outer-space fantasy or mysteries. Don't be discouraged when a writer won't take your suggestion. Just keep suggesting and praising.

• Ask the class to write about a moment in time when they changed. Give examples: "The first time I saw my baby brother." (Note: This could be done orally using the exercise in chapter 1.)

• Ask students to create a made-up character fifty years older who has a problem they have.

• Tell students what risk is. You could define it simply as writing about something you have never written about before or starting at the end and working backwards to the beginning. Ask them to define risk for themselves in writing, then have them explore this new territory in one of their freewrites.

• Take note of what students are writing and model alternative genres through reading out loud to them. Take time to discuss and speculate about published work from the writer's point of view. If possible, expose students to interviews where writers talk about their struggles. Remember that most young writers don't realize how common most problems are.

• Here are a few writing prompts that could get students to take risks:

A. What about writing something that
    scares you?
    confuses you?
    mystifies you?
B. Think of someone you dislike. Pretend you are that person and describe yourself through his or her eyes.
C. Write about a deep sadness.
D. Pretend you are a different creature or inanimate object. Write about life from that point of view.
E. Create a character who has lost something.
F. Write about a personal weakness and a day you had to face it.
G. Write down an insulting name or word that someone in your family has called you. Write about how it made you feel and how you are more than that.

thirteen

Words in Collision

Revising Poems

*A word is dead when it is
said, some say.
I say it just begins to live
that day.*
    Emily Dickinson

When I travel to schools I notice two types of poetry, the kind that kids write and the kind they learn to write. The first, usually written in the younger grades, is full of imagination and life. It surprises you with words and metaphors that take you off guard. The second is flowery, contrived, more like the poetry of greeting cards. It rhymes predictably and seems to contain little of the student who wrote it. I am not blaming teachers for this transition. I think that poets themselves and cultural attitudes toward poetry must shoulder most of the blame. Only poets who teach children have struggled to find ways to unlock the magic of words bouncing off and clinging to each other. The rest have toured the globe, lecturing and reading, often pretending that their power was simply their own god-given secret and they were unable to share it.

Geof Hewitt, a Vermont poet who has taught in the public schools for fifteen years, never mentions poetry when he gives the following exercise to begin his classes. He is acutely aware of the baggage the word "poetry" carries and uses his talents to help students of all ages see the power of poems in their own words, not the words they memorized in an English class.

Here's the exercise Geof created to introduce classes to real poems.

Collaborative Poetry

1. Ask each student to write down a phrase that describes an observation made between awakening this morning and arriving at school. Make sure the class understands what a phrase is. Explain that you don't want them to write "I observed the birds flying," but just, "The birds flying." That's what they write. Just what they observed. They have twenty-two seconds to do this. The goal is to get them to write quickly without thinking or worrying.

2. Ask each student to read their phrase from the page. This is very important because students change things when they don't read exactly what they wrote. A verb-driven phrase, like "the fox runs across the road," can easily become a gerund, like "a fox running across the road," when they say what they wrote.

3. Take dictation, writing one phrase per line on the board,

calling on people at random. Insert your own phrase at random, too.

4. Read the phrases as if they are a poem, then ask the class to define what was just read.

5. Explain that you have just written a collaborative poem and that they have relinquished their copyright to their own individual phrases in order to own the larger body of the poem. Everybody owns the poem now. Ask everyone to copy it down in their notebooks and revise it any way they want to.

6. Model the editing and revising processes right in front of students on the board. Cut out phrases or add words, remove lines or tighten up the syntax. Do anything you want to make your poem better. (Note: there is no guarantee that revision will make the poem better. For this reason it is important to save all drafts of your poetry.)

7. Share the edited poems. Marvel at the differences and similarities.

Here's a list of observations and how Geof Hewitt edited them.

Everybody Down Up

by Geof Hewitt

A lot more stoplights now on route 15
Than in 1968, but there's still that house with the pond!
and Sadie still sits on top of the gravel pile
In damp, blank, closed sky.

Inside that house I know Rilla runs around the room:
"I'm naked, Daddy!" Beautiful mother and daughter,
small birds swoop my windshield
while a squirrel works an apple back up the tree.

distance where I least expected it, once my home
I've got a motel where the showerhead sprays in a circle,
Fog hangs on hillsides and a "Bove and Fagan" ice cream truck
Is what my window looks out on and music plays, everybody up
down.

Here's how I edited it.

Red light 10:00 am June 17th
1991   **by Barry Lane**

A small bird swoops
towards my windshield
Sadie at the top of
the gravel pile,
Damp
Blank
Closed
sky.
I think of
Rilla running
around the room,
last night,
"I'm naked Daddy!"
"I'm naked Daddy!"

Beautiful mother
  and daughter
this morning
at the breakfast table

eating
milk soaked
Cheerios

Outside,
A squirrel works an
    apple back
    up the tree.

   Distance,
   where I least
   expected it.
   Showerhead sprays
   in a circle,
   Fog hangs on
   hillsides

   More stoplights
   on route 15
   than there were in
   1968

It was fun to revise this poem and fascinating to see how I did it differently than Geof and to imagine how someone might take yet a different approach. It's easier and more fun to revise collaborative poems because the words are not your own and because of that they are not glued to feelings and thoughts. We can play with them like toys, assembling and re-assembling them in different ways to create different effects.

Verandah Porche is a poet who has been teaching in Vermont schools for many years. She carries with her a heart-shaped tin box wherever she goes. It contains thousands of words all liberated from their original contexts. There are stories from a fourth grade in Vermont, poems her daughter Emily wrote, the Declaration of Independence, pieces of the I Ching. It is a sort of cornucopia of literature all stuffed into her little box. Tell a class what poetry is, inspire them with wonderful simple poems, give them a prompt to get them started, and students will still sit there, fearful, waiting for divine inspiration.

But tell them you have brought some words for them to play with. Ask them to reach in and grab a few fistfuls, and suddenly they are mixing metaphors, screaming for more words, delighting in an incongruous combination like a Pig in a Wig, or Dad's kissing sad bags.

Children have a natural love for playing with words. No three-year-old would ever say a pun was the lowest form of humor. Yet when it comes to playing on the page, a lack of fluency often interferes with the joy of hooking words together or bouncing them off each other.

Verandah Porche's wordboxing is the single most wonderful way I have found of getting children and adults of all ages to play with words.

Here's how it works.

Wordboxing

1. Make photocopies of books you have read with the class or student stories or anything else you'd want to use. Slice up all the words and put them into your chosen vessel (have the students help if you want). (Tip: It's nice to have words on durable tag board, but quantity is more important than quality. Stuff your box full.)

2. Read students some playful poems and tell them that poets play with words on the page like toys on the floor. Tell them you are going to teach them to do the same. Explain to them that their poems don't have to make sense. They don't have to rhyme (but they can; see spin-off). They don't have to use all the words you give them, and they can trade.

3. After finishing a poem, ask them to write it down before rearranging their words into another poem.

4. The class shares their poems and talks about how poets surprise them.

5. Suggest they try rearranging the same words into another poem.

Like the collaborative poem exercise, wordboxing is a wonderful way to gain distance from poems in order to develop a concept of revision that might not come as readily with our own words, which are firmly attached to our feelings. Once they've unlocked this magic they can return and apply these concepts to the poems they write. Teach the joy of playing with words and phrases and ultimately they will learn the power of poetry.

Spinoffs

- Have students pick nouns, adjectives, and verbs from their individual piles of words. Write a familiar piece of writing on the board, like the Pledge of Allegiance (you might want to pick one less patriotic). Now go through the piece with the class identifying the parts of speech. Erase them and put an N for noun, an A for adjective and a V for verb. (Note: Leave a few words so the piece is recognizable.) Now go around the class revising the piece, taking a word from each student (e.g., "I pledge peanut butter to the salami of underwear.")

Repeat this same exercise with different words.

• Collect a bunch of words that rhyme and make a special wordbox. You may want to have the children write the words. Ask the students to arrange nonsense poems that rhyme.

• Teach students what an image is by using poems. Create an imagebox on a theme (e.g., war and peace). The box will contain written images of war and peace. You could add images from published poets as well.

Each student takes a handful of images and arranges a poem. (Note: This is a great way to teach juxtaposition. You can point to how certain images are stronger when placed next to others.)

• If you have a video camera at your disposal try the first exercise of this chapter by taping close-ups of students' faces as they say what their observations are. Experiment with other forms, such as the concept poem, where a word like *peace* is repeated after five images or peaceful words. (Note: These poems could be created without a camera as group poetry. Experiment with your own forms.)

• Students write a poem that depends on a title to fill in the information like this one:

Ode to a Lost Brain Cell

Where did I put it?
It was here
I know it
Think, Think, Think

• Have students write a poem that is a dialogue between two people. You could model this by starting with one voice and having the class reply. Here's one I wrote with a group of sixth graders recently:

The Messy Room

CLEAN YOUR ROOM!
No way, Jose.

Clean Your Room!
  In a minute.
Clean your room
  What Room?

● Ask students to write a poem that begins with a question they sometimes ask themselves. Here's one that I have: Why do dogs love to roll on dead things? (Don't hesitate to let students explore questions like this, especially if they're adolescents! You'll be surprised at how something that may seem to be a wisecrack at first turns out to be quite interesting.)

When students revise their poems they may want to cut out the question or leave it in. A question can also be a great jumpstart for revising poetry.

● Conduct poetry readings regularly. Here's the best way to do one that I've found. Students stand one to three at a time in front of the class and read their poems. The class must applaud after each poem. Everyone must listen carefully.

● Have students revise "Roses are Red" poems to make them lose the predictable rhyme and get more interesting.

Here are a couple I wrote for a class last Valentine's Day.

Roses aren't red
Violets aren't Blue
If you think poems have
  to rhyme
Think again.

Red Roses
Blue Violets
Sugar stuck to dead words
in my poem
Your eyes and
mine rhyming
Yeah!

(Okay, so they're not great. But they were fun to write, and that's the point.)

● Teach metaphor with this fill-in-the-blank exercise:

_____ is a _____.
(feeling)   (noun)

Anger is a *hissing cat.*

Once students have this sentence they must dig deeper for details to make the image come alive.

● Have students write a poem about a landscape inside them, like this one by seventh grader Erin Williams:

Wishes
Inside me,
There is a world waiting
to be set free
Violet men,
Violet women,
Gazing at the same
Rainbow.
Wondering, wondering,
Each star is a wish,
When will mine come true?

When students are done with one landscape, have them revise their poem by writing another. Have them draw pictures and use crayons to depict their landscapes.

fourteen

Befriending the Language

I do not choose the right word. I get rid of the wrong one.

A. E. Houseman

It happened on a field in East Sussex, England, a town today called, appropriately, Battle. The year was 1066 and the Normans, under the direction of William the Conqueror, were just about to defeat the Anglo-Saxons, who were led by a king named Harold. You can stand on that field today and watch the sheep graze. You can stand in the place where the archers stood three rows deep and imagine that moment when a stray arrow fatally wounded Harold, and the battle ended. History books call the Battle of Hastings the Norman Conquest, the foundation of what we call modern England. Linguists recognize this moment as the birth of the English language, and writers like me see it as the day all the weaker three-syllable Latin words invaded all the strong one-syllable Anglo-Saxon words. I visualize the Normans posturing with determination and advanced emotions of superiority and devotion, while the Anglo-Saxons fight with strength and will and fall one by one in cold blood. As a writer I am always flipping through the William words and searching for the Harold words.

Big words are certainly the weakest ones. Small words have all the clout. That is no doubt why George Orwell came up with his rule, "Never use a big word where a small word will do" (Murray, 162).

Author Richard Lederer says that English poets use 70 percent Harold words and only 30 percent William words. As you might imagine, the same does not hold true for insurance policies or memos from the Pentagon. The English language is full of words that mask meaning instead of clarifying it, yet how often do English teachers point this out?

A mistake we make as teachers is to promote the study of vocabulary as an end in itself. I wish I had a dollar for every student who came to me and said, "I will be a better writer as soon as I get a bigger vocabulary." As a teacher I know that these students have not been taught to value their own words, learned through reading and speaking, but instead taught to believe that all the words in dictionaries and thesauruses are the ones that really matter. Perhaps worse than that, they have been taught that words are like fancy hats they can put on and make things sound better instead of a way to make things clearer.

There is a similar problem with how grammar is sometimes taught. As a writing teacher I always cringe when a student hands me a paper and says, "I put some really good adjectives in that poem. I think you'll like them."

Immediately, I know this is a student who learned that language could be separated from content. I'm not saying there is anything wrong with knowing the parts of speech, but when this knowledge appears to be more important than the writer's message, then it's time to question our priorities. We need to teach grammar and craft, but whenever possible we must teach it in the context of the student's own writing as a means for communication, not an end in itself.

Here are a few fun ways to give students a line-by-line awareness of the power of words without teaching grammar or vocabulary out of a textbook.

Daily Group Editing

Editing is as much a habit as a skill. This is a great way to affirm a class's editing skills and make it fun.

Each morning before your students arrive write a sentence on the board with at least as many errors in it as there are students in your class. Give the sentence some of the problems we have discussed in this chapter and make the content relevant to that day's activities. Students then go up in pairs and each one corrects one error telling the class what the problem was and how they corrected it. Students applaud after each correction.

Name That Gerund: (A Quiz Show)

This is good fun but it takes some preparation. It can be as involved as you want to make it. For example, you could build a set and produce a video to use in other classes.
1. Collect problem sentences from students' work. Have your students do the collecting in their groups. Put all the sentences in a hat.
2. Select several groups to play. The waiting groups become the studio audience. Select a moderator. Either you or an elected group of students are judge. (This is a little risky because it's sometimes hard to get kids to agree, and you need a

sense of absolute authority for this to work. I suggest you be the judge for this reason.)

3. Decide on a scoring strategy. For example: One point if a team rewrites the sentence correctly. One point for each problem the team can name by its proper grammatical name.

The judge decides which answers are acceptable.

4. Play the game and have fun. Create new rules as you go.

Grammar in Progress

Perhaps the most misunderstood aspect of writing process is how to teach grammar and editing. Teachers ask me all the time, "If we don't publish anything, how can I teach editing?" Somewhere along the line a myth developed that freewriting or journal writing should remain exempt from all rules of grammar, spelling, usage, and anything to do with mechanics. Every writer knows that the more you know about grammar and punctuation the more versatile or free your writing can become. Students can still freewrite and be aware and accountable for the grammatical rules and spelling they've learned in class. I'm not saying that students should worry about their grammar while freewriting; rather, like all writers they can go back and self-edit. What better way for writers to learn what paragraphs are than to go back through their journal and create new paragraphs with their editing pen?

Here is a way to teach grammar in everyday journal writing that leaves the students in control.

Contracting for Grammar in Journal Writing

1. Teach a mini-lesson on some aspect of grammar that you've noticed from students' writing needs clarification. (Make sure students know the copyediting symbol for the aspect you are teaching. If you're unfamiliar with these symbols, look at a copy of the *Chicago Manual of Style* and make a chart for your class.)

2. Once your lesson is taught, give students a contract in which they agree to write or edit what they learned. This doesn't mean they have to do it right away. They can go back and self-edit a day's entry, making new corrections with their editor's pen. The contract only means that they are responsible for what they are learning and must apply it because it will help them to learn it better. If contracting seems too formal, create some other format to make your students accountable for the grammar they learn.

3. As students edit their own work for grammar they will suddenly truly begin to learn it. Conduct a seminar later in the year where students pick out some of their favorite sentences or paragraphs where they used what they learned. Display them with favorite sentences and paragraphs from their favorite authors.

4. Follow a similar process or design your own to teach other lessons of grammar. Make students accountable in their own writing for what you teach them and they will truly learn it.

I never learned to enjoy editing my sentences until years after I left school and struggled on my own to become a professional writer. Teachers tried to help me with their correction marks but all I learned was that I made many mistakes. As students write more and teachers feel less responsible for teaching grammar as an isolated skill, the possibility develops for students to gain a more complete appreciation for the way language works.

Invent ways to put your students in control of their grammar. Teach them to delight in the miracle of language.

Here are a few mini-lessons to tune students' red pens to the joys of editing.

Spinoffs

- *Down writing/up writing.* Take a simple eleven-word sentence like "The dog took a bone and hid it under the bed," and ask students to revise it by adding as many words as they can without significantly changing the meaning. This can be done as a contest between groups. You may want to make a rule that prohibits more than three adjectives in a row.

• *Sentence Shrinking.* Find a piece of tangled-up, boring prose from an insurance company or a faculty memorandum. Ask the same groups to rewrite it so a first grader could understand it. Shrink the syllable and word count.

• *One-syllable writing.* This one's for Harold. Students write a description of a place using only one-syllable words.

This often produces some remarkably powerful writing. Point out to students the power of small words.

• *Long sentence, short sentence.* Writers often learn pacing instinctively through their reading, but teachers can help by pointing out the rhythm of sentences. This exercise is simple. Students write about a dramatic moment in a horror story when their character is about to discover something scary. Have them begin their writing with one or two long sentences and end the paragraph with three short sentences. (*Example:* "Giles walked into the hallway, noticing the crystal chandeliers, the gilded wallpaper, the polished imitation marble tiled floor that appeared to be waxed this morning. The scream pierced his brain. He turned to the door. The bullet zipped past his ear. Fear.")

• *The adjective is the enemy of the noun.* (Voltaire). Here's an old journalism trick. Have students go through a piece of writing and cross out every adjective and adverb. Now ask them to revise the piece by finding stronger verbs and nouns. (*Original:* The small two-year-old child quickly moved across the room. *Rewrite:* The toddler scampered across the room.) (Note: The purpose of this exercise is to teach the power of verbs and nouns. Adjectives and adverbs are not intrinsically bad, but it never hurts to question their use.)

• *War on prepositions.* Students circle all prepositions in a piece of writing. (Explain that prepositions are words like *to, at, in.* They often begin and connect phrases.) Have them rewrite the sentences without the prepositional phrases. (*Original:* In the morning he walked down to his house in a melancholy mood. *Rewrite:* The sun looked weak as it rose over the hay field. Clarence trudged home. His toes stubbed up clouds of dust.

• *Search-and-destroy intensifiers.* There are some words that can usually be edited out of writing if they are not crucial to a writer's voice or to the voice of a character. These words are intensifiers—words like *very, really, extremely*. Ask students to go through their work and cross the intensifiers out, noticing how this makes a piece of writing stronger.

- *To be or not to be . . . there's usually no question.* High visibility of the "to be" verb in a piece of writing usually means the author is writing in passive voice or stuck in some tense that is weakening his or her writing. Teach kids to rewrite sentences in passive voice by killing the "to be" verb and by flip-flopping the sentence. (*Original:* The blueberry pie was eaten by Kurt. *Rewrite:* Kurt ate the blueberry pie.)

- *Fighting introductory clutter.* There is a certain breed of word that likes to hang out at the beginnings of sentences in the guise of introduction. Often, these lazy, good-for-nothing words trick writers into thinking they are important when they are really just dead wood. It is important that an editor develop an eye for spotting them and cutting them. Try editing the last three sentences I wrote. Look at all the dead wood you can cut out. Remember Strunk and White's motto: Omit useless words.

- *Owning words.* Ask children to make vocabulary and spelling lists out of their weekly reading across the content areas. Teach kids to administer tests to each other and learn each other's words. Compile all the words each week onto a master list and compare it to vocabulary lists in boring textbooks. Is it different?

- *I-n-g O-U-T!* Sitting at the front of a sentence, an introductory participial phrase often is unnecessary. Using the editing techniques described in this chapter, train students to look for such phrases and cross them out.

When Is It Done?

A poem is never finished, only abandoned.
Paul Valéry (on a bad day)

"Why do writers love writing?" I ask the class.

"They get paid lots of money," one student says.

"Not true," I say. "Out of the thousands of professional writers in this country, only a few hundred have actually gotten wealthy through their writing."

"They like to entertain other people," another student says.

"True," I say, "but isn't it a lot easier to entertain people without having to write it all down."

"They like to tell stories and express their ideas," another student says.

"Why?"

"Because it makes them feel good."

As students learn that writing fulfills the human need of expression, they begin to understand that revision does not have to be a chore. The common language of craft and techniques presented in this book can open students' eyes to the pleasures of revising, to delight in what novelist Bernard Malamud called "the flowers of afterthought." In time this conceptual language of craft will help students revise a piece of writing long after the initial spark of enthusiasm has failed. But when is a piece truly done, or do we expect students to just keep on revising a piece of writing forever? How do students move from revising ideas to revising sentences? How can teachers integrate the teaching of grammar and other editing concerns with a student's quest to finish a piece of writing?

"It's Done!"

If you're a writing teacher who has encouraged revision, you have heard these two simple words many times. It is futile for teachers to impose their authority when a student has reached closure on a piece of writing. However, students can create questions to meditate on before they decide a piece is finished. A question to a writer can be like a toothpick to a baker. It probes and tests to see if it's really done.

Here are a few questions I have developed with students in conferences. Try brainstorming a list with your own students and posting it in the classroom or using it as a conference checklist for students.

Questions to Decide if It's Done

1. Does the lead pull the reader in?
2. Does the piece say what I want it to say?
3. Does the ending grow out of the piece or is it tacked on?
4. What is my favorite part? Why?
5. What is my least favorite part? Why?
6. What would I like to write more about, either in this piece or another?
7. Can I cut words, phrases, ideas?
8. Can I insert snapshots, thoughtshots, or explode moments?
9. Is there a better lead buried in the piece?
10. Does the piece flow?

Once a student decides a piece is done a whole new set of editing concerns comes into play. Sentence-level editing is the finish work, or polishing, of writing. If revision is the process of building and rebuilding the walls of the house, then editing involves sanding and waxing each sentence and paragraph.

"Who Needs More Practice Editing, Your Students or You?"

Though study after study has proven that red penciling every student error does not help students to become better editors many teachers still cling to this method out of fear and a misguided sense of duty. Some teachers limit the amount of writing their classes do because, "How can I find time to correct all those papers?" In some communities where the concepts of process writing has not taken hold, an uncorrected grammatical error in the hand of a parent is like a warrant for the teacher's arrest.

These methods, and the fears that fuel them, developed out of a system that, for historical reasons, only judged writing by its grammatical correctness. This system encouraged safe, expressionless writing, holding up primers and basal readers as models of perfection. But let's stop for a minute and consider the absurdity of this viewpoint in light of a broader assessment of the qualities in writing. Would a teacher feel compelled to add more details to a student's work or infuse it with more purpose or voice before allowing it to be sent home?

As teachers unchain themselves from overblown grammatical expectations, they allow students to start editing their own work. After all, aren't they the ones who really need the practice?

Editing Conferences

A student comes to an editing conference ready to look at their work sentence by sentence. There are many ways of organizing such a conference. Here are a few ideas.

1. Focus the conference on one or two grammatical points learned in mini-lessons over the week. The student comes to the conference with an edited manuscript, having circled all areas where these points apply. Pay particular attention to mistakes the student has corrected.

2. Students come to conference with an unedited manuscript. You hand them a red pen and ask them to focus on one grammatical error at a time as they go through the manuscript (e.g., finding sentence fragments).

3. Ask students to edit one of your rough drafts. If it's like mine there will be many chances to prove their grammatical superiority.

4. Find a wordy but published piece of writing. Make a photocopy and ask a student to edit it for clarity.

5. Invite three students to an editing conference. Give them all a different color pen. Rotate short pieces of unedited writing, either their own or other students. Challenge students to re-edit another student's corrections. Discuss, debate, and explore different ways of editing the same piece of writing.

(Note: As mentioned in chapter 14, a standard chart of copyediting symbols can be found in the *Chicago Manual of Style* or other grammar reference books. Make a chart of these symbols and post it in your classroom.)

Editing Checklist

Making checklists with a class can be a great way of integrating the teaching of grammar, usage, and mechanics with the self-editing skills that will help students their entire lives. Using a checklist is simple. A student takes one or two points on the checklist and checks the entire manuscript in those areas. When he or she is done, that category can be checked off.

What follows is a typical editing checklist. Students should add to the list as mini-lessons in grammar are taught throughout the year and as they discover new problems through their own writing. Here is a sample checklist I made with one of my classes; I suggest you make one with your class and ask students to add to it as the year goes on.

- Circle words I am unsure of. Check spelling.
- Check for correct use of "their," "there," or "know," "no."
- Check that "a lot" is two words; try replacing with "much" or "many."
- Use a semicolon between two sentences that have a relationship.
- Check paragraphing. Break up very long ones or melt together shorter ones if need be.
- Write on one side of the paper so writing can be cut and pasted if need be.
- Use apostrophes to show possession.
- Use capitals at beginnings of sentences and in nouns and adjectives of titles.
- Use a colon to begin a list of things.
- Put a comma after the salutation of a letter and after the closing.
- Split words between syllables.
- Start a new paragraph after a new speaker speaks.
- Keep voice of the story consistent (first, second, or third person).
- Read softly out loud, watching for typographical errors. Make sure each word is read so simple errors aren't skimmed over.

Revisor's Checklist

Students who begin editing may find themselves drawn back into larger revisions. Here is a list of possible directions to send a writer back into a piece of writing. Try brainstorming a similar list with your class after you have taught students many of the techniques in this book and developed some of your own through experimenting in the classroom. Encourage students to add to this list as the year goes on and as they gain experience revising their own work. Keep track of new methods of revision that develop and make a point of highlighting them at writing share time.

- Cross out THE END and write five unanswered questions and turn the most compelling one into a new lead.
- Insert a snapshot.
- Insert a thoughtshot.
- Insert some dialogue or cut some uninteresting dialogue. Build an entire scene.
- Break the story into chapters.
- Break the story into pages using illustrations as your guide.
- Write the story from a different point of view.
- Write the story as a poem. Write the poem as a story.
- Explode a moment.
- Cut writing up into paragraphs. Keep the best ones and throw away the rest. Write the piece again, building on the parts you kept.
- Write a new title.
- Cut ineffective lines of dialogue and replace with snapshots and thoughtshots.
- Find a new lead.
- Cut anything.
- Draw illustrations and see if you can add more detail based on what you draw.
- Read the piece out loud and listen to your voice. Notice the places where you read faster and the places where you slow down. Ask yourself what you can do to change the parts you don't like.
- Go for a long walk or take a shower and think about your story.
- Question Conference with a friend.
- Hide your story in a drawer and forget about it.
- Start something new that grows out of the original story.
- Write a letter to a famous author telling about your story and

your process of writing it. Ask the author how they would deal with certain problems you are facing.

- Write a letter to a friend about your story.
- Write a letter to a character in your story describing a problem you're having writing it.

Forming an Editing Center

Form groups of four to six students. Decide which grammatical problems each group will address. Each group then makes a sign that demonstrates in a sentence which problem is being addressed (e.g., We luv 2 spel grate!!). Ask groups to decide on a system that works for editing papers. One might be that the papers go around in a circle and each person double-checks the other's work. Another system might be that each member edits one paper, initials it, and puts it in a pile in the center to be double-checked by another member. (Note: Though editing centers provide a service for writers who are polishing their work, it may be important to encourage students to self-edit their work first so that they learn to see errors in their own work.)

Creating Criteria for Portfolio Assessment

A writing portfolio is a personal anthology of work chosen by the student. You've probably heard talk of portfolios, and I encourage you to read more about them in order to understand their purpose more fully. Some titles are listed in the bibliography.

Like editors at a publishing house, students must develop their own criteria and learn to judge different qualities in their work. Creating criteria and assessing their own work is a wonderful way for students to reach closure, not only on any given story but on the entire body of their work.

Here's a way to help students create their own criteria:

1. Brainstorm a list of qualities that constitute good writing. You may wish to begin by reading a piece of powerful writing and asking what makes it powerful.
2. Pare down the list, combining qualities into simpler categories. For example, "vivid" and "real" might fall into a category like "details." Look at Vermont's portfolio assessment chart in Figure 15–1 to get an idea of some possible criteria.

Figure 15–1 Vermont Writing Assessment Chart

Vermont Writing Assessment
Analytic Assessment Guide

	Purpose	Organization	Details	Voice or Tone	Grammar/Usage/Mechanics
In assessing, consider...	...how adequately intent and focus are established and maintained (success in this criterion should not depend on the reader's knowledge of the writing assignment: the writing should stand on its own)	coherence: ...whether ideas or information are in logical sequence or move the piece forward ...whether sentences and images are clearly related to each other (Indenting paragraphs is a matter of Grammar/Usage/Mechanics)	...whether details develop ideas or information ...whether details elaborate or clarify the content of the writing with images, careful explanation, parenthetical expressions, stage directions, etc	...whether the writing displays a natural style, appropriate to the narrator ...or whether the tone of the writing is appropriate to its content	...the conventions of writing, including: *Grammar (e.g. sentence structure, syntax) *Usage (e.g. agreement and word choice) *Mechanics (e.g. spelling, capitalization, punctuation)
Ask how consistently, relative to length and complexity...	intent is established and maintained within a given piece of writing	the writing demonstrates coherence	details contribute to development of ideas and information, evoke images or otherwise elaborate or clarify the content of the writing	an appropriate voice or tone is established and maintained	As appropriate to grade level, command of conventions is evident, through correct English or intentional, effective departure from conventions
Extensively	Establishes and maintains a clear purpose and focus.	Organized from beginning to end, logical progression of ideas, fluent and coherent.	Details are pertinent, vivid or explicit and provide ideas/information in depth.	Distinctive personal expression or distinctive tone enhances the writing.	Few or no errors present; *or* departures from convention appear intentional and are effective.
Frequently	Establishes a purpose and focus.	Organization moves writing forward with few lapses in unity or coherence.	Details develop ideas/information; or details are elaborated.	Establishes personal expression or effective tone.	Some errors or patterns of errors are present.
	⌐ Yes ¬	⌐ Yes ¬	⌐ Yes ¬	⌐ Yes ¬	⌐ Yes ¬
	Is author's focus clear within the writing?	*Does the organization move the writing forward?*	*Do details enhance and/or clarify the writing?*	*Can you hear the writer? Or, is the tone effective?*	*Does writing show grade-appropriate command of G/U/M?*
	⌐ No ¬	⌐ No ¬	⌐ No ¬	⌐ No ¬	⌐ No ¬
Sometimes	Attempts to establish a purpose; focus of writing is not fully clear.	Lapse(s) in organization affect unity or coherence.	Details lack elaboration, merely listed or unnecessarily repetitious.	Attempts personal expression or appropriate tone.	Numerous errors are apparent and may distract the reader.
Rarely	Purpose and focus not apparent.	Serious errors in organization make writing difficult to follow.	Details are minimal, inappropriate, or random.	Personal expression or appropriate tone not evident.	Errors interfere with understanding.

NONSCORABLE
* is illegible: i.e, includes so many indecipherable words that no sense can be made of the writing, or
* is incoherent: i.e, words are legible but syntax is so garbled that response makes no sense, or
* is a blank piece of paper
* **For Portfolio:** Does not have required minimum contents

©1994 Vermont Department of Education

3. Establish at least four or five categories and a four-point scale.
4. Assess a piece of writing as a class, voting in each of the categories. If students are off by more than one point, mediate by having each student make a case for the qualities in the writing that made them cast their vote.
5. Draw a graph showing the strong points and the weak points of the piece of writing.
6. Write a letter to the author, beginning with specific praise and incorporating what you've learned from the assessment.

Authentic Assessment—An Alternative to the C +

In 1990, Vermont became the first state in the union to pilot portfolio assessment as its means of assessing educational growth. Years ago, when a parent asked a teacher "How is my child doing in writing?" the teacher would take out standardized test scores, worksheets, and the occasional theme about summer vacation. The parents would get numbers and skill sheets that ranked their child, but they learned very little about how that child had integrated those skills into his or her own writing. Today, in Vermont, parents get handed a portfolio, with dated pieces of writing as well as reading journals. They see that in September, Johnny was not using commas correctly but in February, he was, or that in September, Jane wrote with little detail but in December, one story had elaborate description of a bird soaring over her family's neighborhood, and an opinion piece on the Brazilian rain forest was backed up with a slew of concrete facts.

Unlike standardized tests, which often only prove that a child can think like someone in Princeton, a portfolio is a window into a student's learning and can be as useful to the student as to the teacher. For this reason Vermont's students are asked to write a letter about their best piece and include it in their final portfolio. There are a few directions I've found useful to writers grappling with a letter about their writing.

Writing Letters About Your Work

- Describe the process of writing this piece from beginning to end. Where did you add things? Where did you cut?
- Tell the parts you like the best and why?

- How is this piece the same or different from the work you have done in the past?
- Is this piece risky for you? Describe any other stories or pieces that might grow out of this piece.
- Was your personal writing process the same for this piece as others or was it different? Describe.

Many assessors in Vermont remarked that the students' letters about their best piece illustrated how a student's ability to write well about his or her personal writing process went hand-in-hand with the powerful writing they produced. When a student is struggling to finish a piece of writing we must always remember that understanding the struggle is as important as the final draft.

All writers love to finish stories, but in the end they are always more excited about the stories they haven't told yet. Finding new ways to tell and retell these stories is why writers love writing.

Spinoffs

- Students create a personal anthology of their favorite poems, short stories, or essays. Have them assess these stories using the same criteria they assess their own work by.
- Give students an old basal reader to assess with their criteria for good writing. Note the qualities of lifeless prose.
- Students pick their best piece of writing to date and write a detailed letter about their process of writing it. They can follow some of the guidelines above or wing it.
- Ask students to cut ten words out of a finished story. They share cuts with each other in small groups and illustrate how trimming out extra words makes writing stronger.
- Begin a writers' workshop by having every student in the class write a letter to the featured writer (one of the students). The letter must begin with some specific praise about the piece and must be signed. Discuss the story, making sure the writer is in charge. This can be done by having an author's chair at the front of the classroom and insisting that the author be prepared to ask questions and tell the audience what type of criticism she wants. Pass all the letters to the writer.

sixteen

The Writing Doctor

Index to a Few Writing Ailments

...I knew this would be a long night. The patient was riddled with embedded clauses and comma splices. Gerunds clung to his sides and participles dangled from his shoulders as he collapsed on the table.

from the journal of a Writing Doctor

When I was in graduate school I had a humorous advice column in the English Department newsletter called "The Writing Doctor." (At least some people thought it was humorous.) It was sort of a cross between William Strunk, Woody Allen, Ann Landers, and Dr. Timothy Johnson. I have forgotten most and lost all of the pieces I wrote, but I remember one particular piece where I described surgically removing several insubordinate clauses from a Sociology Ph.D. candidate's thesis in an all-night ordeal that left the floor of the operating room littered with commas, colons, and gerunds.

When I think back to what I wrote in the column I realize that much of the humor lay in the self-importance of surgeons being juxtaposed with the comparatively trivial world of the English teacher correcting a paper. It has often puzzled me why doctors get so much more respect than teachers in our society. All doctors really do is patch a few wounds and maybe cure a few diseases. Teachers are responsible for helping to form the ideas, thought processes, and moral fiber of the next generation; but go to most towns in America and you find they are underpaid, maligned for having summers off, and viewed by many as a babysitting service.

Even more puzzling to me is how the attitudes toward education don't mirror the attitudes towards medicine. Nobody longs nostalgically for the days of the one-room hospital where they lopped off limbs instead of treating infections with antibiotics, but many people say they long for the one-room schoolhouse, where students' imaginations and self-esteem were lopped off in favor of boring primers and insulting, mindless, drill-and-kill instruction.

If you ask me, the main problem with American education is a fundamental lack of respect for teachers. It is reflected in their salaries, their self-concept, and the way they are treated by administrators, school board members, and parents.

Since I perceive no immediate change in the future, I have responded in protest by becoming a doctor for the rest of this book. Doctors are paid more and are highly respected by society. They also have the added advantage of sending a bill each time a patient comes to see them, whether the patient gets healed or not. Some of them are so wealthy they even take the summers off!

I invite you to become a Writing Doctor with me, your colleagues, and also your students. Establish your own clinic and consult with each other. Help to cure writing diseases by following and adding to the prescribed remedies.

Some Common Writing Ailments and Prescriptions (Index to Writing Problems)

Then and Then Pox (Chronologititus—Latin)

Symptoms: Writer writes the same way he or she live, one moment at a time. Everything is included because it happened that way. Stories and essays often resemble laundry lists of events, with little differentiation between the death of Grandpa and purchase of a pack of Chiclets. The word "then" is used frequently.

Prescription: Illustrate to patient that writing is different than living. Model the writer's power of choice. Teach how writers can make an impact by expanding one brief moment in time to cover pages. Show the joy of leaving stuff out. (See chapters 1, 4, 5, 6, 11.)

Favorite quote: "I like to leave out the parts readers skip over." (Elmore Leonard)

Placebo Paper Syndrome (SoWhatitus—Latin)

Symptoms: The writer appears to have little or no reason to be writing the piece other than to please somebody or receive a grade. There is a general lack of focus or a strange feeling of detachment in the writing. It could be written by a Pentagon spokesman or an insurance salesman. It could be written by anyone—but not the lively person you know.

Prescription: Ask "Why are you writing this?" Ask writer to make a list of questions that the piece does not answer. Call a press conference where the entire class turns into reporters. Find out the *rest* of the story and if it's not there, encourage the writer to find other subjects. (See chapters 1, 2, 6, 7, 9, 10, 12).

Favorite quote: "All writers are vain, selfish, and lazy, and at the very bottom of their motives there lies a mystery." (George Orwell)

Blocked Passages (Blankslatitus—Latin)

Symptoms: Writer recoils at the mention of the term freewriting. Writer appears tired and listless during writing sessions. Writer writes without passion or clarity. Writing seems more a fine motor skill than a tool for thinking. When cornered the writer says she has writer's block.

Prescription: Assure writer that there is nothing wrong with her. Find quotes from other writers about getting stuck. Call a writer's symposium where classmates reveal techniques for getting unstuck. Assign special topics or exercises that may have a liberating effect. Writing short prose poems can be such an exercise, or wordboxing (you cut up stories into words and make poems out of the words you pick out of a box; see chapter 13). Teach the writer to write without touching pen to paper. Describe how Wallace Stevens wrote poems while walking to work. (See chapter 9.)

Favorite quote: "Writing is long periods of thinking and short periods of writing." (Ernest Hemingway)

Delusions of First-Draft Grandeur (Reluctant Revisititus—Latin)

Symptoms: Writer feels no need to revise any of his writing except to spell words right. Writer's eyes glaze over when the word "revision" is mentioned in conference.

Prescription: Teach writer that writing *is* revision. Use leads and details to help the writer find new angles on his piece. Demonstrate the joy of inserting snapshots, thoughtshots, and scenes. Explode moments. Always assure the writer that it may not be time to revise this piece yet. Let it sit. Also remember, you don't have to write it over to revise it.

But before you make any suggestions praise what is there. (See chapters 1, 2, 3, 4, 5, 6.)

Favorite quote: "It ain't over till it's over." (Yogi Berra)

Dialogue-arhea (Looses-lipsus—Latin.)

Symptoms: Writing suffers from an excess of flat dialogue that doesn't move the story along.

Prescription: Replace dialogue with exposition and insert mini-snapshots and thoughtshots to make real scenes. (See chapters 3, 4.)

Favorite quote: "In art, economy is always beauty." (Henry James)

Bouts of Vagueness

Symptom: Writing gets vague in places for no apparent reason.

Prescription: Conference and ask writer to describe the areas where writing is vague. Determine if the vagueness is a result of missing detail or an unsure purpose. Vagueness is often a necessary stage for writers who are exploring uncertain territory. Suggest inserting snapshots or thoughtshots. Where could they go? (See chapters 1, 2, 3, 7.)

Favorite quote: "If you cannot find it within yourself where will you go for it?" (Confucius)

Micro-mania (computer-addictictus: Latin)

Symptom: Student refuses to write or revise unless she can use the computer. Unfortunately there are twenty other students sharing the same computer.

Prescription:

1. Send student to a model school where they have re-placed teachers and have one computer per child.
2. Threaten to send her to the same school.
3. Get an extra job so you can afford to buy a computer for this student.
4. Teach student to revise without writing it over. Teach techniques like inserting snapshots, cutting and pasting, exploding moments. Unless you have computer time each day for each student, that computer will be nothing more than a typesetting machine.

Favorite quote: "A writer who waits for ideal conditions under which to work will die without putting a word to paper." (E.B. White)

Deathless Prose (Superhero-sillius: Latin)

Symptom: This subject-related affliction occurs often in the work of young writers who write seething, endless adventure stories that are often infected with chronologitius.

Prescription: Ask the writer what the hero's problem is. Ask if there are any moments to explode in the story. Suggest that the writer insert a thoughtshot of the hero at a crucial part of the story. Suggest telling the story from the monster's point of view. (See chapters 1, 2, 3, 5.)

Favorite quote: "I'd be golden if it wasn't for that darn Kryptonite." (Superman)

Lined with Rhyme (Roses-are-Redus, Violets-are-bluesis—Latin)

Symptom: Poems suffer from too many convenient, life-depleting rhymes.

Prescription: Teach writer that poems don't have to rhyme. Read them William Carlos Williams' poetry. Teach poets the joy of playing with words. (See chapter 13.)

Favorite quote: "Poetry is fewer words that say more." (Barry Lane)

Stuck Poems (Oracle-itus—Latin)

Symptom: Poet refuses to revise any of his poetry because it doesn't feel right to do so.

Prescription: Model more radical forms of revision, like the shotgun revision in chapter 9. Illustrate that you can turn a poem into a story and a story into a poem. Try the image-shuffling poem in chapter 13. Revise group poems. Revise published poems. Don't enforce revision. Give the writer the tools and let the writer decide.

Favorite quote: "Like an ice cube on a hot stove a poem must ride on its own melting." (Robert Frost)

Blurry Vision (Fuzzy-itus: Latin)

Symptom: Writer has a lot to say but everything she writes down is fuzzy and hard to get a handle on.

Prescription: Teach writer to dig for details and practice writing snapshots regularly. Illustrate how to insert snapshots into stories. (chapters 2, 3, 8)

Favorite quote: "There are significant moments in everyone's day that can make literature." (Raymond Carver)

Vanished Voice (Research-Paper-Laryngitus: Latin)

Symptom: Student seems unable to write a research paper without regressing to the mechanical voice of an encyclopedia.

Prescription: Teach students to follow their own curiosity when doing research. Show them how to choose facts that intrigue them most and follow the most interesting questions. Insist that they find a lead that compels them to write on. Show them that even encyclopedias are not objective sources. They have a point of view. (See chapter 11.)

Favorite quotes: "There are important differences between women and men beyond the primary fact that women are the mothers of men."

"Man: (see human being)."

(the definitions for *woman* and *man* in the 1968 *World Book Encyclopedia*)

Fear of Flying (Congenital-scriba-phobia—Latin)

Symptom: Student refuses to do anything but the assignment you have given and then only does the bare minimum. When questioned he tells you he hates writing.

Prescription: Find ways to alter student's expectation of what writing is. Avoid forming your own expectations of the student's writing ability. Keep trying new things and wait to be surprised. (See chapter 12.)

Favorite quote: "Teach yourself to work in uncertainty." (Bernard Malamud)

Uncut Words (Editophobia/ Editomalaise: Latin)

Symptom: Student is afraid to edit her own work or is bored with editing.

Prescription: Find ways to make editing both routine and fun. (See chapters 14, 15.)

Favorite quote: "I'm not alone when I'm writing—the language itself, like a kind of trampoline, is there helping me." (William Stafford)

Dead Air (Conferencinoma: Latin)

Symptom: Peer conferences do little to improve student's writing.

Prescription: Establish a format in your classroom that puts the student in control. (See chapter 7.)

Favorite quote: "Craft is perfected attention." (Robert Kelly)

Processed Writing (Verbal Velveeta-itus—Latin)

Symptom: Student's writing follows all the steps of the writing process but lacks any enthusiasm or sense of discovery.

Prescription: Teach student that writing is like digging potatoes. Show student how to grow leads from real questions. Explore the power of digging for details to find focus and meaning. Show students how to graph and map ideas to find the place of tension and meaning before they even begin writing. Find ways to make it more fun. (See chapters 1, 9, 11.)

Favorite quote: "Writers write for the same reason readers read—to find out what's going to happen." (Elmore Leonard)

Dr. Lane's Ten Rules for Revising Our Concept of Revision
(There Are Twelve Because I
Already Started Revising Them)

1. Be more interested in what is *not* on the paper.
2. Ask questions that make the writer want to tell and write more.
3. Understand that one method of revision is to write a new paper.
4. Use leads and details to help writers find a focus.
5. Develop strategies that fit the writer's individual and personal needs.
6. Pay attention to the writer's revising process and find methods, such as interviews, to make him or her aware of it.
7. Don't ask writers to revise everything they write. Rather, teach them that writing *is* revision.
8. Never be afraid to be critical. Know when to be a tough editor and when to be a nurturing teacher. Remember that too much unqualified praise can be as damaging to a writer as flat rejection. Focus your criticism to one or two points.
9. Never tell a writer a paper is done. Always point out more suggestions for revision. Remember Valéry's observation, "A poem is never finished, only abandoned."
10. Find methods to put writers in charge of grammar and spelling problems. Who needs more practice editing, your students or you?

11. Encourage the peer group revision process where possible. Let the students be their *own* best critics, but give students critical guidelines to follow.

12. Revise and break these rules when possible. Create some of your own with your class.

Atwell, Nancie. 1987. *In the Middle: Writing, Reading, and Learning with Adolescents.* Portsmouth, NH: Heinemann.

Babbitt, Natalie. 1975. *Tuck Everlasting.* Toronto: Collins.

Ballenger, Bruce, and Barry Lane. 1989. *Discovering the Writer Within.* Cincinnati: Writer's Digest.

Carver, Raymond. 1983. "A Small, Good Thing." In *Prize Stories: O. Henry Awards 1983.* New York: Doubleday.

Charlton, James. 1984. *The Writer's Quotation Book.* New York: Penguin.

Chicago Manual of Style. 1982. Chicago: U of Chicago P.

Freedman, Russell. 1987. *Indian Chiefs.* New York: Holiday House.

Hansen, Jane. 1987. *When Writers Read.* Portsmouth, NH: Heinemann.

Hinton, S. E. 1988. *Taming the Star Runner.* New York: Delacorte.

Márquez, Gabriel García. 1976. *One Hundred Years of Solitude.* New York: Avon.

McInerney, Jay. 1984. *Bright Lights, Big City.* New York: Vintage.

McPhee, John. 1966. *Oranges.* New York: Farrar, Straus & Giroux.

Murray, Donald M. 1990. *Shoptalk: Learning to Write from Writers.* Portsmouth, NH: Heinemann-Boynton/Cook.

Orwell, George. 1950. *Shooting an Elephant and Other Essays*. New York: Harcourt Brace Jovanovich.

Paterson, Katherine. 1987. *The Great Gilly Hopkins*. New York: Harper & Row.

Paulsen, Gary. 1987. *Hatchet*. New York: Puffin.

Rico, Gabrielle Lusser. 1991. *Pain and Possibility*. Los Angeles: Jeremy Tarcher.

Smith, Frank. 1988. *Joining the Literacy Club*. Portsmouth, NH: Heinemann.

Speare, Elizabeth George. 1983. *Sign of the Beaver*. New York: Dell.

Spinelli, Jerry. 1990. *Maniac Magee*. New York: Scholastic.

Strickland, Bill. 1989. *On Being a Writer*. Cincinnati: Writer's Digest.

White, E. B. 1952. *Charlotte's Web*. New York: Harper & Row.

Wilder, Laura Ingalls. 1971. *Little House in the Big Woods*. New York: Harper & Row.

Zinn, Howard. 1980. *The People's History of the United States*. New York: Harper & Row.

In addition to the books I've listed in the text and in the Works Cited section, following are books that I've found to be helpful in both my teaching and personal writing. I share them with you in hopes that you'll find them to be useful as well, in your quest to learn and discover, both professionally and personally.

Books on Learning to Love Writing

Discovering Your Own Literacy by Donald Graves. (Portsmouth, NH: Heinemann, 1989). Graves knows teachers are busy people who don't always have time to write. This book shows some helpful ways of incorporating writing, reading, and learning with your students into your lives.

Writing Down the Bones by Natalie Goldberg. (Boston: Shambala, 1987). Inspiring bits of wisdom that you can read in small chunks and that make you want to pick up a pen.

Writing the Natural Way by Gabrielle Lusser Rico. (Los Angeles: Tarcher, 1984). A nice introduction to writing as a right-brained activity.

Books on the Writer's Craft

The Art of Fiction by John Gardner (New York: Vintage, 1982). This inexpensive paperback is packed with useful theory and good exercises.

Creating the Story: Guides for New Writers by Rebecca Rule and Susan Wheeler (Portsmouth, NH: Heinemann, 1993). A wonderful resource for any teacher interested in writing and teaching fiction. Offers scores of inspiring exercises for writers to practice their craft. Inspirational, thorough, and downright compelling.

The Handbook of Poetic Forms by Ron Padgett (New York: Teachers and Writers Collaborative, 1987). A useful reference for mini-lessons on teaching poetic form.

Writers at Work series, edited by George Plimpton (New York: Penguin, ongoing). Interviews with well-respected writers of all generations taken from the *Paris Review.* This series represents some of the most interesting examples of how all writers think and write differently.

Books on Implementing Student-Centered Learning and Writing Process in Your Classroom

The Curious Researcher by Bruce Ballenger (New York: Allyn & Bacon, 1992). Ballenger does not believe the research paper has to be boring for either the writer or the reader. This book is a must for the junior high and high school teacher who wants to break out of the boring report syndrome.

Essays into Literacy by Frank Smith (Portsmouth, NH: Heinemann, 1983). Frank Smith's essays in this collection shatter many myths about how students learn to read and write.

Learning by Teaching: Selected Articles on Writing and Teaching by Donald M. Murray (Portsmouth, NH: Heinemann-Boynton/Cook, 1982). Murray is a journalist first and a theoretician second. That's why his scholarly essays on writing are so fun and inspiring to read.

Invitations: Changing as Teachers and Learners, K–12 by Regie Routman (Portsmouth, NH: Heinemann, 1991). Everything a teacher interested in holistic, learner-centered teaching could want to know, including the famous "blue pages" section at the end of the book, full of suggestions for further reading as well as sample forms to use in the classroom and more. Routman deals with the realities and difficulties teachers face as they move toward change in their educational philosophy, since she is a teacher herself.

Reading Without Nonsense by Frank Smith (New York: Teachers College Press, 1982). This book clearly illustrates the need to teach students how to read for meaning.

Write from the Start: Tapping Your Child's Natural Writing Ability by Donald Graves and Virginia Stuart (New York: NAL-Dutton, 1987). Convincing parents of the importance of holistic instruction can sometimes be an awesome task. This inexpensive, wonderfully written paperback will help clear the way for you.

Writing: Teachers and Children at Work by Donald Graves (Portsmouth, NH: Heinemann, 1983). Still the seminal work on writing process in the elementary school, Graves's book is full of great examples of how to help empower students.

Writing to Learn: How To Write & Think Clearly About Any Subject at All by William Zinsser (New York: Harper Collins, 1988). Zinsser illustrates how writing can be a tool for learning across the curriculum.

Books on Assessment and Portfolios

Evaluating Literacy: A Perspective for Change by Robert Anthony, Terry Johnson, Norma Mikelson, and Alison Preece (Portsmouth, NH: Heinemann, 1991). A practical book written for teachers interested in holistic, learner-centered methods of evaluation and assessment, this title offers teachers both a clear understanding of what's involved as well as gives concrete suggestions for implementing the theory into practice.

Portfolio Assessment in the Reading-Writing Classroom by Robert J. Tierney, Mark A. Carter, and Laura E. Desai (Norwood, MA:

Christopher Gordon, 1991). A wonderful, well-researched book that defines the whys and hows of portfolios. Sure to be a classic.

Portfolios: Process and Product edited by Pat Belanoff and Marcia Dickson (Portsmouth, NH: Heinemann-Boynton/Cook, 1991). A collection of essays about different uses of portfolios in a broad range of classrooms. Full of suggestions for teachers beginning to use portfolios with their own students.

Portfolio Portraits edited by Donald Graves and Bonnie Sunstein (Portsmouth, NH: Heinemann, 1992). A collection of essays, written by teachers of different grade levels as well as researchers in the field. Illustrates the different ways we can think of portfolios, and urges us to think more carefully about why they're effective rather than merely jumping on the portfolio bandwagon.

Books on Selling Your Writing

Children's Writers and Illustrators Market (Cincinnati: Writer's Digest, published annually). Full of names and addresses of editors and agents in the children's publishing world, as well as tips on publishing children's books, stories, and articles. A wonderful resource to have in the classroom and in your personal library.

The Children's Picture Book: How to Write It, How to Sell It by Ellen E. Roberts (Cincinnati: Writer's Digest, 1987). This book has some good, solid advice that will help you present your children's book to a publisher.

How to Write a Book Proposal by Michael Larson (Cincinnati: Writer's Digest, published annually). Book proposals are easy to write and a way to sell a nonfiction idea before you write a book. This short book is written by an agent who has seen and sold many proposals. It's full of good tips that could (so what if the odds are high?) get you a job for your summer vacation.

Writer's Market (Cincinnati: Writer's Digest, published annually). The unquestioned Bible of the freelance writer, this book is full of addresses of magazines, book publishers, and agents to send your work—whether it's fiction, nonfiction, or poetry—and start your journey toward publication.

This book does not present a step-by step method, but an evolving process, and you and your students are part of that process. I'd love to hear how the ideas within these pages have translated into your classroom. Drop me a line and let me know.

Barry Lane
Discover Writing
RR 1 Box 142
Shoreham, VT 05770
phone: 802–897–7022

index